Alexa Skills Projects

Build exciting projects with Amazon Alexa and integrate it with Internet of Things

Madhur Bhargava

BIRMINGHAM - MUMBAI

Alexa Skills Projects

Commissioning Editor: Gebin George
Acquisition Editor: Divya Poojari
Content Development Editor: Eisha Dsouza
Technical Editor: Sneha Hanchate
Copy Editor: Safis
Project Coordinator: Shweta H Birwatkar
Proofreader: Safis Editing
Indexer: Rekha Nair
Graphics: Jisha Chirayil
Production Coordinator: Nilesh Mohite

First published: June 2016

Production reference: 1290618

Published by Packt Publishing Ltd.
Livery Place
35 Livery Street
Birmingham
B3 2PB, UK.

ISBN 978-1-78899-725-6

www.packtpub.com

Dedicated to everyone who is taking their first steps in learning about voice computing. May the force be with you.

`mapt.io`

Mapt is an online digital library that gives you full access to over 5,000 books and videos, as well as industry leading tools to help you plan your personal development and advance your career. For more information, please visit our website.

Why subscribe?

- Spend less time learning and more time coding with practical eBooks and Videos from over 4,000 industry professionals
- Improve your learning with Skill Plans built especially for you
- Get a free eBook or video every month
- Mapt is fully searchable
- Copy and paste, print, and bookmark content

PacktPub.com

Did you know that Packt offers eBook versions of every book published, with PDF and ePub files available? You can upgrade to the eBook version at `www.PacktPub.com` and as a print book customer, you are entitled to a discount on the eBook copy. Get in touch with us at `service@packtpub.com` for more details.

At `www.PacktPub.com`, you can also read a collection of free technical articles, sign up for a range of free newsletters, and receive exclusive discounts and offers on Packt books and eBooks.

Contributors

About the author

Madhur Bhargava is specialized in Wireless and Mobile Computing from CDAC ACTS Pune, India. He started his career at Electronic Arts as a software engineer working on mobile games. He later addressed problems in personalized healthcare, leveraging the power of mobile and voice computing. He is proficient in various mobile/embedded technologies and strives to be a software generalist. He believes that good software is a result of talented individuals working together as a communicative team in an Agile manner. He likes to spend time with his family, read, and watch movies.

I would like to thank my family and the team of amazing people I am working with. They are the reason that made this book happen.

About the reviewer

Srini Janarthanam is an expert in Chatbots, NLP and AI technologies with over 10 years of experience. He got his Ph.D. from The University of Edinburgh. He worked as a researcher at Edinburgh and Heriot-Watt Universities where he worked on several research projects and authored over 50 conference/journal publications. He runs a chatbot and AI solutions agency - Chatomate. He recently authored the book *Hands On - Chatbots and Conversational UI Development* published by Packt.

Packt is searching for authors like you

If you're interested in becoming an author for Packt, please visit `authors.packtpub.com` and apply today. We have worked with thousands of developers and tech professionals, just like you, to help them share their insight with the global tech community. You can make a general application, apply for a specific hot topic that we are recruiting an author for, or submit your own idea.

Table of Contents

Preface

The advent of voice computing in recent years has caused a tectonic shift, with the result being that interactive voice-based personal assistants no longer lurk in the shadows, and Amazon Alexa, Siri, and Google Now have become common household names. Apart from their traditional abodes of mobile devices, these assistants can also be found in the center of our living and dining rooms in the form of Amazon Echo, Google Home, and Apple HomePod devices.

This book focuses on harnessing the power of voice computing by studying Alexa, which is the interactive voice-based personal assistant used in Amazon Echo. Over the course of this book, we will embark on a journey to understand the internals of Alexa and how it works under the hood, while creating five unique Alexa Skills, each of which will be designed to address a specific purpose and a real-world use case.

I hope you enjoy the journey!

Who this book is for

This book is aimed at everyone who is interested in learning about the underlying voice computing technology on which Amazon Echo and Alexa are based, and also learning how we can leverage that technology to create skills for Alexa oriented towards home automation, the Internet of Things, and various other domains.

What this book covers

Chapter 1, *What Is Alexa?*, is an introductory chapter that does not require any coding skills. We discuss how intelligent voice-activated personal assistants are evolving from just being passively present in mobile phones to becoming a permanent fixture in common households in the form of dedicated hardware devices.

Chapter 2, *Hello World, Alexa!*, will introduce the reader to the process of creating skills for Alexa and will explain how to create a basic Hello World Alexa skill.

Chapter 3, *Hands-Free Experience with Alexa*, will introduce a new way of sending messages using Alexa, that is, the hands-free way.

Chapter 4, *Let's Play Factly with Alexa*, will create a game called Factly as an Alexa skill. We will also add persistence to it using DynamoDB.

Chapter 5, *Making Alexa Talk about CryptoCurrencies*, will demonstrate how Alexa can provide the latest cryptocurrency updates. The user will create an Alexa skill that can fetch the current prices of the latest cryptocurrencies, such as Bitcoin and Ethereum.

Chapter 6, *Home Automation with Alexa*, will demonstrate how Alexa can integrate with other IoT devices and create the foundation of a smart home. The user will create a Weather Monitor Alexa skill that can inform the user about the climate (temperature/humidity/light) in the home.

Chapter 7, *Future of Voice-Based Personal Assistants*, will talk about the future of the intelligent voice-based personal assistants.

To get the most out of this book

The following are the prerequisites to get the most out of this book:

- Basic familiarity with a modern programming language such as JavaScript. All of the code that we'll write for the Lambdas is based on Node.js.
- Free Tier Amazon AWS Developer account.
- Basic familiarity with code editors.
- Not mandatory, but recommended is an Amazon Alexa-enabled device, such as an Amazon Echo.
- Over the course of this book, we will be making many configuration changes via the Amazon Developer Portal. We recommend that you follow these steps as described, so a good Internet connection is highly recommended.

Download the example code files

You can download the example code files for this book from your account at www.packtpub.com. If you purchased this book elsewhere, you can visit www.packtpub.com/support and register to have the files emailed directly to you.

You can download the code files by following these steps:

1. Log in or register at `www.packtpub.com`.
2. Select the **SUPPORT** tab.
3. Click on **Code Downloads & Errata**.
4. Enter the name of the book in the **Search** box and follow the onscreen instructions.

Once the file is downloaded, please make sure that you unzip or extract the folder using the latest version of:

- WinRAR/7-Zip for Windows
- Zipeg/iZip/UnRarX for Mac
- 7-Zip/PeaZip for Linux

The code bundle for the book is also hosted on GitHub at `https://github.com/PacktPublishing/Alexa-Skills-Projects`. In case there's an update to the code, it will be updated on the existing GitHub repository.

We also have other code bundles from our rich catalog of books and videos available at `https://github.com/PacktPublishing/`. Check them out!

Download the color images

We also provide a PDF file that has color images of the screenshots/diagrams used in this book. You can download it here:
`http://www.packtpub.com/sites/default/files/downloads/AlexaSkillsProjects_Color Images.pdf`.

Conventions used

There are a number of text conventions used throughout this book.

`CodeInText`: Indicates code words in text, database table names, folder names, filenames, file extensions, pathnames, dummy URLs, user input, and Twitter handles. Here is an example: "On the console search bar, please search for `Lambda`, and click on it when it appears in the list of auto-suggestions."

A block of code is set as follows:

```
buildSpeechletResponse = (outputText, shouldEndSession) => {
  return {
    outputSpeech: {
      type: "PlainText",
      text: outputText
    },
    shouldEndSession: shouldEndSession
  }
}
```

When we wish to draw your attention to a particular part of a code block, the relevant lines or items are set in bold:

```
generateResponse = (speechletResponse) => {
  return {
    version: "1.0",
    response: speechletResponse
  }
}
```

Bold: Indicates a new term, an important word, or words that you see onscreen. For example, words in menus or dialog boxes appear in the text like this. Here is an example: "Select **System info** from the **Administration** panel."

Warnings or important notes appear like this.

Tips and tricks appear like this.

Get in touch

Feedback from our readers is always welcome.

General feedback: Email feedback@packtpub.com and mention the book title in the subject of your message. If you have questions about any aspect of this book, please email us at questions@packtpub.com.

Errata: Although we have taken every care to ensure the accuracy of our content, mistakes do happen. If you have found a mistake in this book, we would be grateful if you would report this to us. Please visit www.packtpub.com/submit-errata, selecting your book, clicking on the Errata Submission Form link, and entering the details.

Piracy: If you come across any illegal copies of our works in any form on the Internet, we would be grateful if you would provide us with the location address or website name. Please contact us at copyright@packtpub.com with a link to the material.

If you are interested in becoming an author: If there is a topic that you have expertise in and you are interested in either writing or contributing to a book, please visit authors.packtpub.com.

Reviews

Please leave a review. Once you have read and used this book, why not leave a review on the site that you purchased it from? Potential readers can then see and use your unbiased opinion to make purchase decisions, we at Packt can understand what you think about our products, and our authors can see your feedback on their book. Thank you!

For more information about Packt, please visit packtpub.com.

1
What is Alexa?

"I definitely saw some power in voice. It's a very powerful form of storytelling."

– Akilah Bolden-Monifa

For our human ancestors, as their brains evolved, so did their language, from signs and sounds to a more sophisticated form of oral speech, which made them capable of having complex conversations to form the social ties required for their survival. Unlike written communication, oral speech leaves no traces of its own, hence it was hard for historians to calculate an exact date for the origin of speech. However, using various methods, historians have speculated that speech was developed 300,000 years ago, symbols 30,000 and writing 7,000 years ago. Ever since then, humans have been putting speech and voice to various creative uses.

In this chapter, we shall explore one such use of our voice, the ability to command interactive voice-based personal assistants to perform specific tasks at will. Also before that, we will also understand what an intelligent voice-based personal assistant is, what needs it fulfills, and what voice-based personal assistants are available (including Alexa) in the current market by going through the following topics:

- The Need for Voice-Based Personal Assistants
- Applications of Voice-Based Personal Assistants
- A Comparison of Various Voice-Based Personal Assistants

So, let's move on to our first topic.

The Need for Voice-Based Personal Assistants

To understand the evolution of voice-based personal assistants, we will have to go back in time and see some of the important events that led to their advent. One of these many events was the evolution of computers. Although not directly related to the voice revolution, the evolution of computers played a key role in the evolution of voice-based personal assistants because it marked the invention of the internet, which is the backbone of most voice-based personal assistants. The computer revolution also introduced critical changes concerning hardware and integrated circuits, which we shall discuss next.

The computer revolution began in the 19th century when Charles Babbage invented the first analytical engine, which earned him the nickname the *Father of Computers*. The 1950s and 1960s were interesting times, which introduced some tremendous advances in the field of computer science with a groundbreaking invention, integrated circuits. Integrated circuits replaced diodes and vacuum tubes, which led to tremendous form factor changes in existing computers, in turn leading to smaller, more compact sizes. It was also the time when Gordon Moore introduced his famous observation that the number of transistors in an integrated circuit doubles every two years; roughly speaking, we would be able to pack more and more processing power into an integrated circuit while the size of the circuit would shrink every two years. Moore's observation already foresaw the future of our technology and hardware, and by following it we could have easily predicted at least one thing, that we would be seeing our computers getting smaller, a lot smaller, and voilà, today nearly everyone has a small computer in his/her hands, their smartphone.

The late '60s and early '70s also saw the advent of the **Advanced Research Projects Agency Network** (**ARPANET**), which eventually evolved to become the internet as we came to know it in the '80s. All this sounds trivial at first, before you realize that all these were the key factors that, had they not been invented, we would have never seen voice-based personal assistants in action.

Prior to voice-based personal assistants, the traditional way of sending commands to a computer system was either through the GUI using a mouse or through the terminal using a keyboard. As the form factor of traditional computing systems reduced, the input methods evolved too and initial handheld devices/mobile phones introduced a stylus in addition to the traditional keyboard to leverage the touchscreen capabilities of the device:

Figure 1.1: A smartphone with a stylus, captured in the year 2010

The evolution continued and the place of the stylus was taken by, as pointed out by Steve Jobs,"the best pointing device in the world," our fingers.

 Steve Jobs introduced touch on the iPhone by using the term "best pointing device in the world" for a user's fingers in 2007 during the MacWorld Conference in San Francisco. The highlights of this conference are available on YouTube
at `https://www.youtube.com/watch?v=P-a_R6ewrmM`.

As the interface between computers and humans grew thinner, it was only natural that voice was the next medium that could act as an input tool to computing devices, and hence there has been the advent of voice-based personal assistants.

 The idea of having voice as an input medium for computing devices was not new; parallel to the computer revolution, there was also the voice revolution, many important discoveries of which are shown in the link: `https://voicebot.ai/2017/07/14/timeline-voice-assistants-short-history-voice-revolution/`

Of the many milestones of the voice revolution, almost every reader will be familiar with at least a few of the latest ones, namely Siri, Google Now, Cortana, and Amazon's Alexa. The most popular ones are Apple's Siri and Google's Google Now, which initially appeared integrated with iOS and Android mobile devices, respectively.

Apple's Siri initially appeared as an app on Apple's App Store, but was later acquired by Apple and became much more closely integrated with iOS devices. Siri uses a natural language interface to listen to commands from the user and perform the necessary actions. Also, with the coming of macOS Sierra, its capabilities were no longer limited to iOS devices:

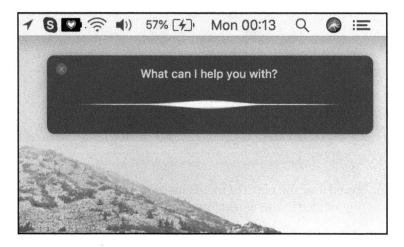

Figure 1.3: The capabilities of Siri also extend to desktops in addition to iPhones

Google closely followed in the footsteps of Apple and, shortly after the introduction of Siri in 2011, introduced Google Now in 2012. Unlike Siri, Google Now was available natively for Android and also as a separate app for iOS devices. Google Now seamlessly integrated with other Android/Google features such as Gmail, Google Calendar, and the mighty Google Search itself:

Figure 1.4: Google Now is available on iOS as part of a native app (Google and the Google logo are registered trademarks of Google Inc., used with permission.)

Closely behind Google was Microsoft with its own intelligent voice-based assistant, Cortana, which it introduced in 2014 for desktop and mobile devices:

Figure 1.5: Microsoft's Cortana was initially introduced for Microsoft's mobile and desktop computing systems

As time passed, it became evident that voice-based personal assistants were here to stay and needed exclusive hardware and space of their own. This was something that Amazon took the lead on with the introduction of its brand Amazon Echo, which was a device family of smart speakers, specifically designed and developed by Amazon Inc. to enable its users to use the services of an interactive voice-based personal assistant called *Alexa* (hence the title of the chapter):

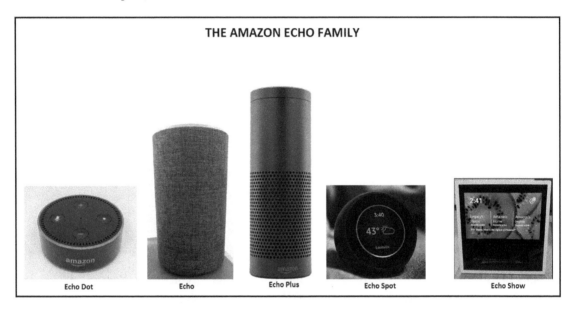

Figure 1.6: The Amazon Echo device family

The complete Echo family and their functionalities are described in the following table:

Device	Use
Amazon Echo	Original flagship smart speaker.
Echo Dot	Smaller and cheaper version of Echo without the amplified speaker, so the sound quality is also inferior to Echo.
Echo Plus	Latest version of Echo with Zigbee integration.
Echo Show	Alexa-enabled device with a large touchscreen so that a user's interaction with Alexa is not just auditory but also visual.
Echo Spot	*Show+Dot=Spot*. All the basic functionality of Show and Dot devices with the much lesser form factor.
Amazon Tap	Alexa-enabled Bluetooth speaker.

The Echo family marked Amazon's second foray into the hardware domain, the first being its introduction of the popular ebook reader, Kindle. Google also recognized the fact that interactive voice assistants can do much more by specifically leveraging the smart home concept and closely followed behind Amazon with its Google Home Smart Speaker, which contained Google Assistant as Alexa's counterpart:

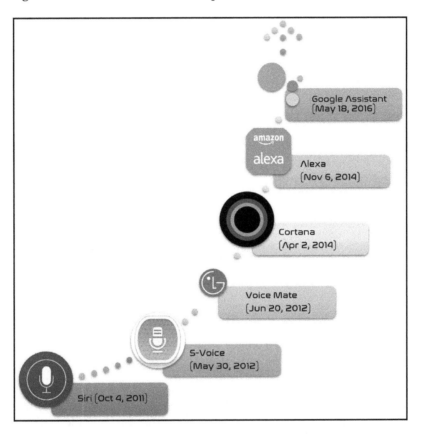

Figure 1.7: Launch timeline for various voice-based personal assistants (source: www.citiusminds.com)

Please note that the preceding diagram does not include Google Now, which was introduced in 2012.

We have discussed the evolution of voice-based interactive personal assistants and how they developed from just another app on the user's smartphone to the user's smart home.

In the next section, we shall discuss some of the popular uses of voice-based interactive personal assistants.

Applications of Voice-Based Personal Assistants

We discussed the evolution of voice-based personal assistants in the previous section. In this section, we shall extend that discussion to some of the popular uses of each of the interactive voice-based personal assistants, irrespective of whether the assistant in question is desktop, smartphone, or smart home-based. We shall begin with one of the earliest and most well-known ones, Apple's Siri.

Siri

As indicated earlier, Siri started as a separate smartphone app in 2011 for iOS, which was later on acquired by Apple. Initially, the capabilities of Siri were limited to smartphones and simple functions such as:

- Looking up contacts
- Messaging (SMS)
- Fetching weather updates on user demand, plus other simple queries as mentioned in the previous section

However, Apple's roadmap also extended the capabilities of Siri by closely integrating it with third-party apps and, true to their promise, with the coming of iOS 10, Apple also released SiriKit.

 To know more about SiriKit, please visit `https://developer.apple.com/sirikit/`.

If the user has the following third-party apps installed, he/she can request a ride using Siri:

- Uber
- Lyft

If the user has the following third-party apps installed, he/she can set those to send a message (and not just an SMS) using Siri:

- WhatsApp
- LinkedIn
- WeChat
- Slack

A user can also make VoIP calls using the following apps via Siri:

- Skype
- Viber

 Please note that the preceding lists are not exhaustive. However, third-party integrations were not the only thing on Apple's roadmap to extend the capabilities of Siri. The launch of macOS Sierra also brought the capabilities of Siri to the desktop. To know more about Siri's desktop capabilities, please visit `https://support.apple.com/en-us/HT206993`.

Siri can also help a user to:

- Search files on his/her Mac
- Notify the user about their storage space
- Send requests to **FaceTime** with **Contacts**, and many others as shown here:

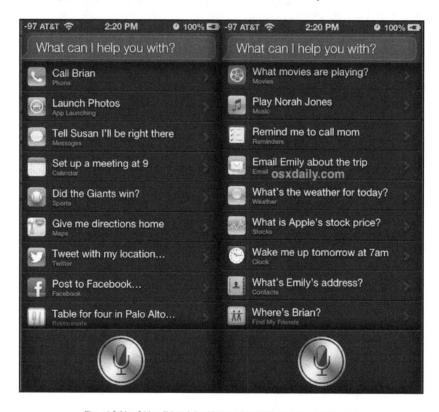

Figure 1.8: List of things Siri can help with (non-exhaustive) (source: www.osxdaily.com)

With a fair idea about Siri's desktop and smartphone capabilities, let's now move on to another popular voice assistant.

Google Now

We are going to discuss the Android and Google Now next, which at the time of writing is the biggest player in the smartphone market and also the home of Google Now, the voice assistant introduced by Google for Android smartphones in 2012.

In early 2010, the smartphone market was dominated by many players. Over the years, this has filtered down and only two major players remain in the market as depicted as follows:

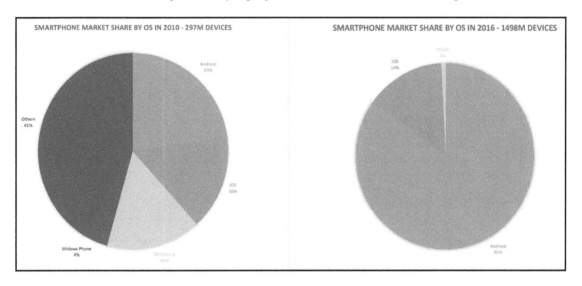

Figure 1.9: Smartphone market share distribution comparison between the years 2010 and 2016 (Data sourced from Gartner)

Google Now can do pretty much all that Siri can accomplish; however, it has better integration with the web and web-based queries, since the web is Google's main forte. Some of the things that a user can ask Google Now are:

Categories	Commands
General commands	• "What is [Schrodinger's cat]?" • "Who invented [the internet]?" • "Post to Google+ [feeling great]"
Notes and reminders	• "Set alarm for [8 PM]" • "Note to self: [I parked my car in section D]"
Time and date	• "What is the time zone of [Berlin]" • "Time at home" • "Create a calendar event: [Dinner in restaurant] [Saturday at 8 PM]"
Communication	• "Call [Daniel]" • "[Contact name]" • "Send [email] to Daniel, [Subject: Meeting], [Message: Will be there in 5]"
Weather	• "Weather" • "Is it going to rain [tomorrow/Friday]" • "How's the weather in [Boston] on [Wednesday] going to be?"
Maps and navigation	• "Map of [Flagstaff]" • "Navigate to [Berlin] on car" • "Show me the nearby [restaurant] on map"

Figure 1.10: Some of the things that Google Now can do (Data source: www.cnet.com)

Apart from Google Now, Google also has introduced Google Assistant, which is a more evolved version of Google Now, given the fact that the user can hold full-length conversations with Google Assistant, which is not possible with Google Now.

It is very likely that Google Now will be phased out and Google Assistant will take its place; however, Google Assistant is currently only available on Google Home, which is Google's smart home speaker; the Android Pixel 2 smartphone; and for Android Wear:

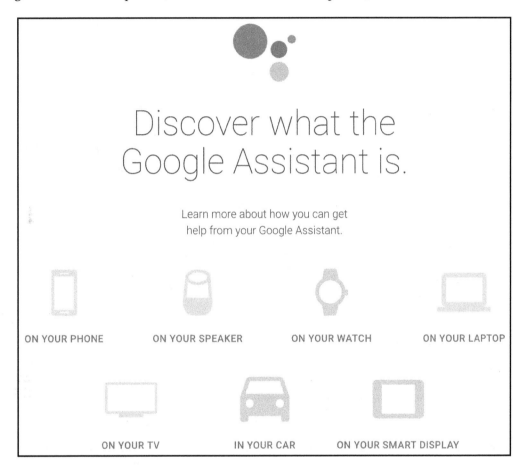

Figure 1.11: Devices on which Google Assistant is available (Google and the Google logo are registered trademarks of Google Inc., used with permission.)

Now, moving on from the smartphone market to the desktop market:

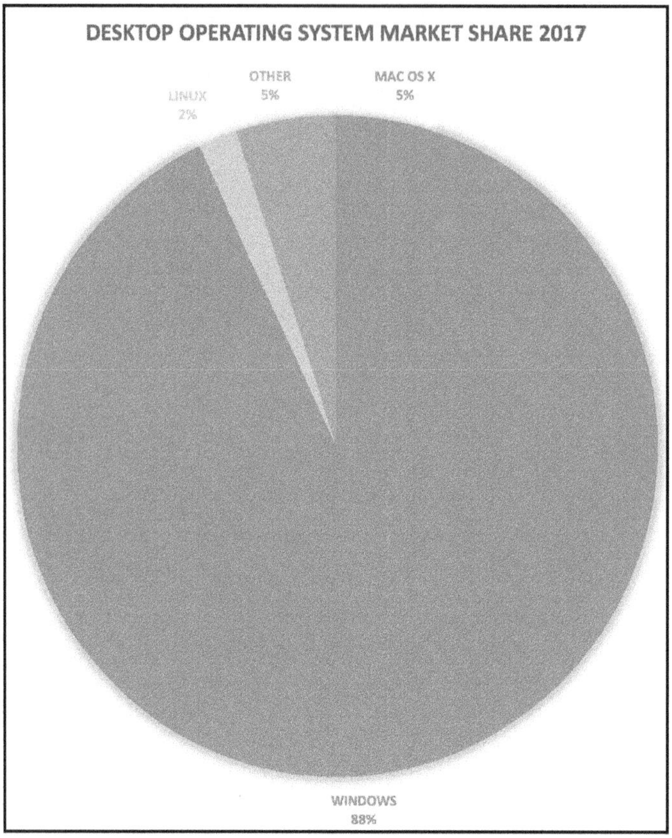

DESKTOP OPERATING SYSTEM MARKET SHARE 2017

OTHER
5%

LINUX
2%

MAC OS X
5%

WINDOWS
88%

Figure 1.12: Desktop market share as of January 2017 (Data source: www.windowscentral.com)

As shown in the preceding graph, as of January 2017, the desktop market had Windows, Linux, and Mac OS X as major players, with Microsoft being the dominant force, which brings us to our next personal assistant.

Cortana

With Microsoft's clear dominance of the desktop market, we cannot ignore Cortana, which is Microsoft's answer to Siri and Google Assistant, but focused on desktop and Windows Mobile:

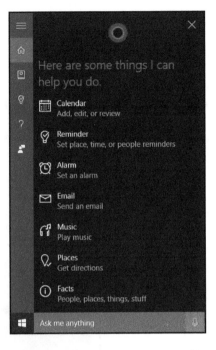

Figure 1.13: List of some things that Cortana can help with

Not just limited to Windows 10, Windows 10 Mobile, and Windows Phone 8.1, Cortana is also available for:

- iOS (as a separate app)
- Android (as a separate app)
- Xbox One
- Invoke smart Bluetooth speaker by Harman Kardon

Some of the many things that Cortana can accomplish are:

- Web-based queries using Bing Search (for example, "Who is the President of the United States?")
- Launch apps and turn on/off Wi-Fi/Bluetooth
- Ask about weather
- Manage appointments, reminders, and events

With that, we come to discuss the Star of this book.

Alexa

Alexa, the whole center point of this chapter and the book, is the interactive voice-based personal assistant by Amazon, originally introduced with its family of Echo devices. Alexa as an assistant is oriented towards a smart home concept, hence most of its use comes from Amazon Echo, a smart speaker designed and developed to be kept in the living room of the user's home so that the user can ask it day-to-day queries about weather, food recipes, and jokes, or play interactive trivia games, set alarms, shop for day-to-day items, and much more. The following diagram shows some of the things that a user can ask Alexa:

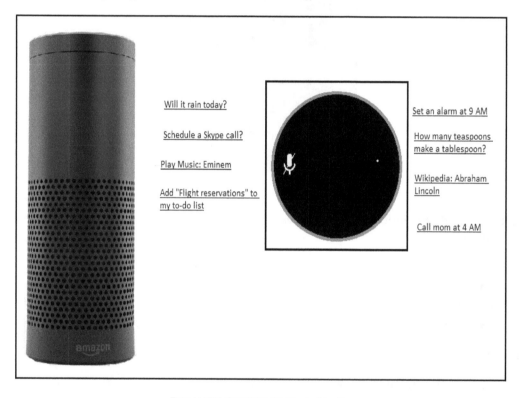

Figure 1.14: List of some things that Alexa can help with

The capabilities of Alexa can also be extended by installing third-party *skills* (similar to Google Home's third-party apps). Each third-party skill is meant to serve a specific purpose. For example, the Uber skill allows you to order a ride, the Domino's skill allows you to order a pizza—all from the comfort of your home and through the magic of your voice working together with Alexa.

As of the time of writing this, there are more than 15,000 skills available for Alexa with Uber and Lyft being the most used ones in the travel category, Pandora and Spotify for music streaming, and multiple other skills being utilized in home automation.

A Comparison of Various Voice-Based Personal Assistants

Due to our previous discussions, we already know that each market, whether it is desktop, smartphones, or smart homes, has a steady supply of interactive voice-based personal assistants. Almost every assistant can do whatever its counterparts can accomplish, but this leads to the question, where do the actual differences lie? Is there something that Alexa can do better than Google Assistant or vice versa?

This book is based on Alexa, which is a Smart-Home based personal assistant, so in this section, we shall compare Alexa and Google Assistant to understand the finer differences between the two:

Alexa	Google Assistant
Uses the invocation phrase, "Alexa"	Uses the invocation phrase, "OK, Google"
Flagship hardware—Amazon Echo device family	Flagship hardware—Google Home, Pixel 2, Android Wear
Responds slightly better to e-commerce/shopping-related queries, since that is Amazon's main forte	Responds slightly better to web-based queries since Google's major forte is web searching
Slightly inferior contextual awareness	Better contextual awareness, hence conversations seem a little more natural
Capabilities of Alexa can be extended by installing third-party "skills"	Capabilities of Google Assistant can be extended by installing third-party apps; however, it has fewer apps currently available for it in the market than Alexa has skills
A wider range of integration with smart home devices such as smart lights, smart locks, smart switches, and smart thermostats	Slightly narrower range of integration with smart home devices

In a nutshell, both Google and Alexa are very skilled voice-based assistants and accomplish a lot for their users; however, since Google Assistant is fairly new to the market, its integration and compatibility with third-party apps and hardware is still evolving, albeit at a very rapid pace. However, even being the newer of the two, Google Home still fares better in terms of web integration and contextual awareness.

It would be really interesting to see what the evolution of AI and Machine Learning brings to the table in the coming era and how these assistants are able to leverage that.

Summary

In this chapter, we covered the evolution of interactive voice-based personal assistants and the various factors involved in their move from a user's smartphone to their smart home. We also saw the various interactive voice-based personal assistants in the smartphone, desktop, and smart home markets, and the capabilities of each.

Our goal was to get the reader familiar with the history of interactive voice-based personal assistants so that over the course of the book, we can direct our focus onto Alexa, the interactive personal assistant bundled with Amazon Echo. The next chapter will enable the reader to understand the anatomy of an Alexa Skill and to hands-on program an Amazon Echo so that Alexa can learn to say one of the oldest phrases in computer programming, "Hello, World."

2
Hello World, Alexa!

"The human voice is the organ of the soul."

– Henry Wadsworth Longfellow

In the previous chapter, we discussed the evolution of various voice-based personal assistants, discussed the capabilities of each of those, and finally compared two significant smart home-based personal assistants, namely Alexa and Google Home.

In this chapter, we will focus on Alexa. We will first learn about Amazon Echo, the smart speaker from Amazon, which enables a user to interact with Alexa and its various flavors. Later on, we will move on to learn about the anatomy of Alexa and what goes into making Alexa so interactive. We will do so by covering the following topics:

- An Introduction to Amazon Echo
- Anatomy of an Alexa Skill
- Building a Hello World Alexa Skill

We will start by introducing Amazon Echo, then move on to the finer details of Alexa and Alexa Skills.

An Introduction to Amazon Echo

Often, the term Amazon Echo is used synonymously with Alexa. However, although both are interrelated, they point to very different things—Amazon Echo is the actual smart speaker (hardware), which is a gateway to Amazon's Alexa Skills service via an interactive voice-based personal assistant.

Amazon Echo has a whole device family and hence comes in many flavors, all of which are discussed in the following sections.

Amazon Echo – First Generation

Amazon Echo was the original first generation flagship smart speaker from Amazon. It requires a wireless internet connection to work as its voice capability (Alexa) is based on a cloud computing service by Amazon:

Figure 2.1: A first generation Amazon Echo

The initial setup of Amazon Echo can be done via the Alexa mobile app, available for both of the major mobile platforms (iOS and Android) and can also be done via the Alexa web portal.

To enable it to reach users of varied economic capacities, Amazon has introduced Amazon Echo Dot, which is a smaller and cheaper version of Amazon Echo:

Figure 2.2: A first generation Amazon Echo Dot

Echo Dot serves the purpose of being a cheaper alternative with a smaller form as compared to the original flagship smart speaker, Echo. To justify the higher cost of the original Echo speaker, it does boast crisp sound and voice control when compared to Echo Dot.

Now, moving on to the second generation of Amazon Echo family.

Amazon Echo – Second Generation

The second generation of the Amazon Echo family introduced newer Echo devices, such as Echo Plus, Echo Show, and Echo Look. Our main focus in this chapter is on the speakers, Amazon Echo and Amazon Echo Dot:

Figure 2.3: Amazon Echo 2, the second generation of the Amazon Echo speaker

Although the second generation Amazon Echo has the same functionality as that of the first generation version, it boasts a crisper sound quality, a smaller form (the second generation Echo is almost two-thirds of the size of the first one), and of course, not forgetting, the fabric skin.

The second generation of the Echo device family also gives Echo Dot an overhaul, as depicted in the following diagram:

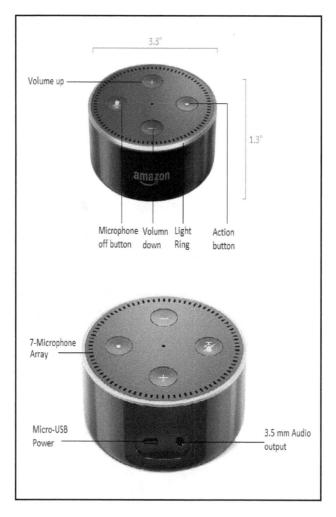

Figure 2.4: Echo Dot second generation version

The major change, as you will notice, is the introduction of two extra buttons for volume control rather than the ring-based control on the older model. Also, the slots for the microphone array have been slightly enlarged for better sound quality, bundled together with a power indicator.

Over the course of this book, we will be mostly using Amazon Echo Dot to test the skills that we create.

 Please do not worry if you do not have access to an Amazon Echo device. There are other ways to test skills, which do not involve buying the Echo hardware devices. We will be introducing these over the course of this book.

If you already have an Amazon Echo or if it is feasible for you to buy one to test the sample skills that we will write (although, as indicated earlier, we have other ways to test skills), then it involves a simple process to set it up, that is, to connect your Amazon Echo to the internet and start issuing commands to Alexa as shown in the following diagram:

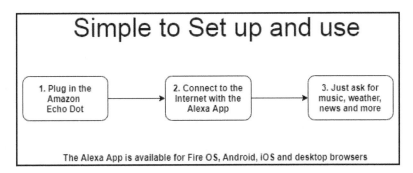

Figure 2.5: Amazon Echo Dot Setup

Hopefully, by now, you should have a clear understanding of what Amazon Echo actually is and of the clear distinction between Amazon Echo and Alexa. In the next section, we will look under the hood of Amazon Echo and dissect an Alexa Skill.

Anatomy of an Alexa Skill

In this section, we will strive to understand what makes Alexa, the personal assistant bundled with Amazon Echo, so smart. The sole reason that Alexa can follow and understand a user's voice commands is because it has *skills,* and not just in a literal sense, but also in an actual sense.

An Alexa Skill is an actual piece of software code designed for a singular purpose; that is, to make Alexa accomplish a certain task. The following are some examples:

- There is an Alexa Skill to order pizza from Domino's Pizza
- There is an Alexa Skill to summon Uber
- There is an Alexa Skill to order flowers
- There is an Alexa Skill to listen to your horoscope

The number of skills available for Alexa has been steadily growing since 2016. As of early 2018, there are over 30,000 third-party skills available for Alexa in the US alone:

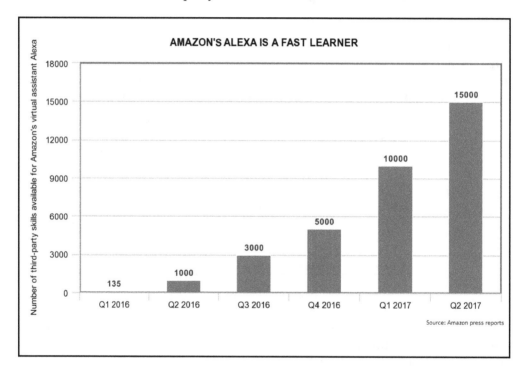

Figure 2.6: Growth statistics for Alexa's third-party skills

Once the user has configured the Amazon Echo device, as shown in the previous section, installing/enabling an Alexa Skill is just a matter of navigating to the Alexa app or Alexa Desktop Portal and selecting the user's favorite skill:

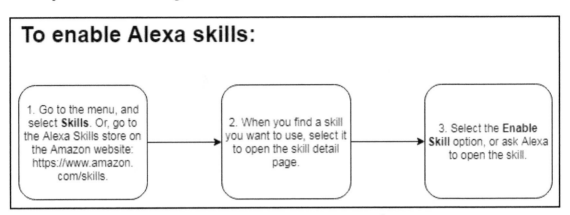

To enable Alexa skills:

1. Go to the menu, and select **Skills**. Or, go to the Alexa Skills store on the Amazon website: https://www.amazon.com/skills.

2. When you find a skill you want to use, select it to open the skill detail page.

3. Select the **Enable Skill** option, or ask Alexa to open the skill.

Figure 2.7: Finding skills via the Alexa mobile app – open the app, select Skills, search for the skill, and click Enable

In a similar manner, a user can disable an already activated Alexa Skill by navigating to the **Your Skills** section from the **Skills** side menu in the app and choosing **Disable**.

To put it simply, Alexa Skills can be compared to educational specializations. As a user installs an Alexa Skill on Echo, he/she is specializing Alexa in a particular task. In the rest of this chapter, we will gain an understanding of how an Alexa Skill achieves specializations.

At the heart of every Alexa Skill are the following components:

- Invocation name
- Intents and Slots
- Lambda

We will discuss each of these separately.

Invocation Name

An Invocation Name is a name that the user of a skill will speak and Alexa will use it to summon or identify your skill from its list of enabled/available skills. An example of a sample skill invocation is shown in the following screenshot:

Figure 2.8: Launching a skill using an invocation name

Please note that in the preceding example, we are using a one-word invocation name, which *normally* isn't allowed by Alexa unless the invocation name is unique to your brand/IP. In the case of Spotify, this is true. Amazon has defined various rules regarding invocation names and these can be found on the Amazon Developer Portal.

 Please navigate to the following link to learn about the invocation name requirements imposed by Amazon for Alexa: `https://developer.amazon.com/docs/custom-skills/choose-the-invocation-name-for-a-custom-skill.html`.

Following the aforementioned rules for an invocation name in an utterance, another sample skill invocation utterance as shown in the following screenshot:

Figure 2.9: Anatomy of a skill invocation name

Hence, every Alexa Skill must have an invocation name and, in the upcoming section, our Hello World Alexa Skill will have one, too.

Intents and Slots

The word *Intent* is derived from intention and, true to its meaning, an intent may map to one or many functionalities of an Alexa Skill. To understand intents better, let's map this to something we already know, that is, common action buttons. For example, an e-commerce app or a web page may have a **Buy** button and clicking on that button will result in a **Buy Action**. When designing for voice, this **Buy Action** will translate into **Buy Intent**. We will look at common usages of **Buy Intent** shortly.

Some intents/actions/functionalities are common to almost every skill, hence they are already predefined/pre-configured for each Alexa Skill. For example:

- Help Intent
- Cancel Intent

 To get more information about built-in intents, please visit `https://developer.amazon.com/docs/custom-skills/standard-built-in-intents.html`.

Each intent has a unique name and a mapping of sample utterances. As a developer, you may ask: *Why the sample utterances?* And, the reason is very simple—designing for voice is a bit tricky, since the user can say multiple things for a single action/intent. For example, for a buy action/intent, a user may say/utter the following:

- Buy *[item-name]*
- Purchase *[item-name]*
- Acquire *[item-name]*
- Go for *[item-name]*
- Hold *[item-name]*

To tackle this, we have utterances of an intent. The more utterances an intent has, the easier it is to invoke it.

Hopefully, you will have a fair understanding of intents by now and that brings us to **Slots**: if an intent is an action, then slots are arguments to that action. In the "buy action/intent" example previously mentioned, the *item-name* will be the argument for the buy intent, hence *item-name* is a slot. We shall see how slots work together with intents in the coming chapters.

Lambda

Lambda is a serverless computing service from **Amazon Web Services** (**AWS**). If this sounds like a lot of technical jargon, please do not be confused as we will be discussing Lambda in detail in this section.

In the context of voice design for Alexa, we will use AWS to host our *core programming logic* in the form of a Lambda function. Now, the obvious question is, *How does Lambda work together with an Alexa Skill?*. To answer, each of the intents/actions on the Alexa Skill will trigger the Lambda function, the Lambda function will process those intents, and this will result in returning an appropriate response for an action/intent, as depicted in the following diagram:

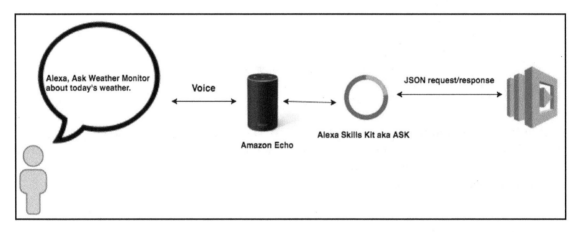

Figure 2.10: Data flow to and from a Lambda

The way this works is as follows:

1. The user utters a voice command/query: "Alexa, ask Weather Monitor about today's weather."
2. Alexa identifies the skill to be launched from the query, which in this case is *Weather Monitor*.
3. Alexa identifies the associated intent based on the utterance: "*ask* [skill name] *about today's weather.*"
4. The intent is identified by the skills kit and is routed to the Lambda.
5. Lambda processes the intent and returns an appropriate response.

At a basic level, almost all Alexa Skills work through the preceding five steps. In the next section, we will actually see these five steps in action as we write our first skill.

Hello Alexa – Building a Hello World Alexa Skill

This section addresses the final goal of this chapter, that is, actually writing our first Alexa Skill. However, please note that we do have a few prerequisites before we embark on the final leg of our journey through this chapter. For the success of this exercise, each user will need to have an **Amazon Developer account**. Signing up for an Amazon Developer account is a simple and straightforward process. The user can sign up for an account at `https://developer.amazon.com`.

Signing up is a three-step process and includes providing personal information, accepting terms of service, and providing a payment method.

 Please note that although signing up requires you to provide Amazon with a payment method, Amazon will charge you if, and only if, you end up using any of the paid services. However, over the course of this book, we will be restricting our usage to free tier and will not be using any of the paid services.

Signing up for an Amazon Developer account not only gives you access to the **Alexa Skills Kit** but also to a plethora of other different services by Amazon, such as AWS and many others. Once you are successfully logged in, you can see all the services that are available to you via the dashboard:

Figure 2.11: Amazon Developer account dashboard (source: developer.amazon.com)

With our signing-up process complete, we can now embark on our journey to create our first Alexa Skill:

1. Please click on the **Developer Console** option button, located in the top-right corner of the screen of the available services dashboard, as shown previously.

2. Once you have navigated to the **Developer Console**, please select the option **Alexa Skills Kit** from the list of options mentioned in the top bar, as shown in the following screenshot:

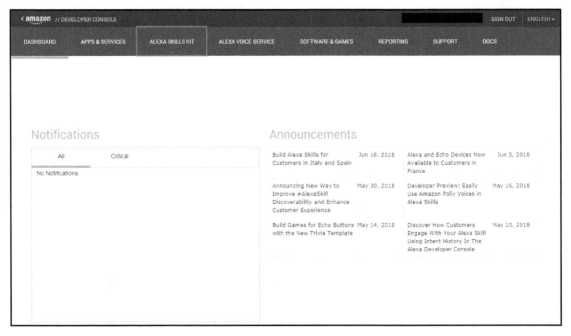

Figure 2.12: Alexa Skills Kit dashboard (source: developer.amazon.com)

3. Please select the **Create Skill** button from the screen that comes up:

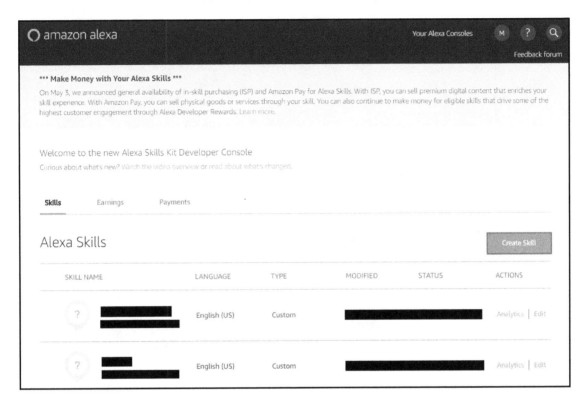

Figure 2.13: Alexa Skills Kit: adding a new skill (source: developer.amazon.com)

4. On the next screen, that is, the **Create a new skill** screen, please provide the skill with a name, as shown in the following screenshot:

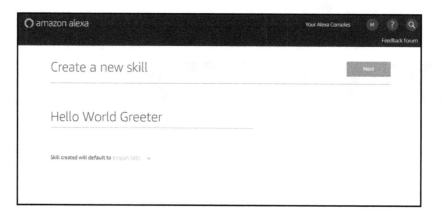

Figure 2.14: Skill name (source: developer.amazon.com)

In our case, we will be using the name `Hello World Greeter`. This is the name that the users see when they are browsing for various Alexa Skills in the Skills store.

Please move on to the next screen, which is the model selection screen, by using the **Next** button:

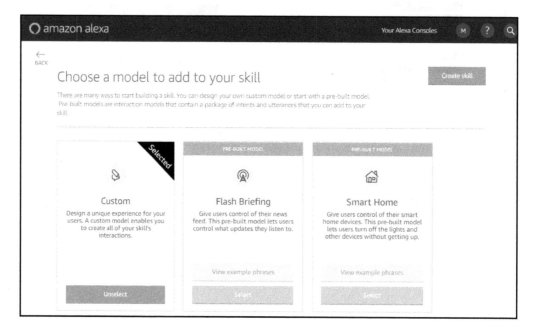

Figure 2.15: Choosing a model for the skill (source: developer.amazon.com)

Please select the **Custom** model for the skill and click on the **Create skill** button in the top-right corner of the screen:

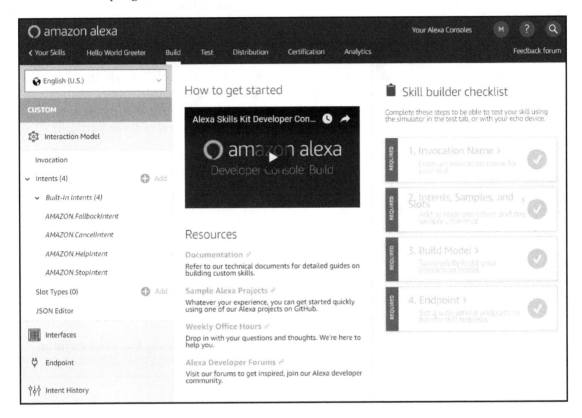

Figure 2.16: Skills dashboard and Skill builder checklist (Source: developer.amazon.com)

This should land us on the skills dashboard shown in the preceding screenshot. As shown previously, the skills dashboard will help us to configure our skill by completing the four steps shown in the **Skill builder checklist**.

5. For our current skill, the functionality is quite simple:

    1. The user invokes the skill by using the invocation name
    2. The user asks Alexa/skill to greet him/her
    3. Alexa responds by saying a predefined greeting phrase

Once we have defined the way in which our skill will work, we will translate the aforementioned steps into something known as an interaction model. Simply speaking, the interaction model is the way in which the user is supposed to interact with your skill. An interaction model is comprised of three parts:

- **Invocation name**: This is the name that the users use to invoke our skill. In our case, we will be using the same value for both the name and invocation name: `hello world greeter`.
- **Intent(s)**: The specific action to be invoked.
- **Slot(s)**: Optional parameter(s) to the action.
- **Sample Utterances**: A list of various things that a user can possibly say/utter to invoke an action/intent.

Since our current skill is very basic it just has a single intent/action and returns a predefined response it does not make use of slots.

We will be configuring the **Interaction Model** by completing the **Skill builder checklist**.

We will begin by defining an **Invocation Name** first.

6. Please click on the **Invocation Name** section under the **Skill builder checklist** to land on the following screen:

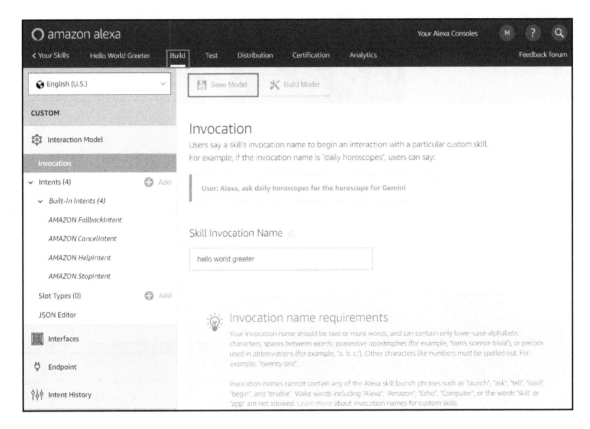

Figure 2.17: Setting up an invocation name (source: developer.amazon.com)

Please add the invocation name as `hello world greeter`, as shown previously, and click on the **Save Model** button to save the changes. After doing so, please click on the **Build** button to land on the **Skill builder checklist** again:

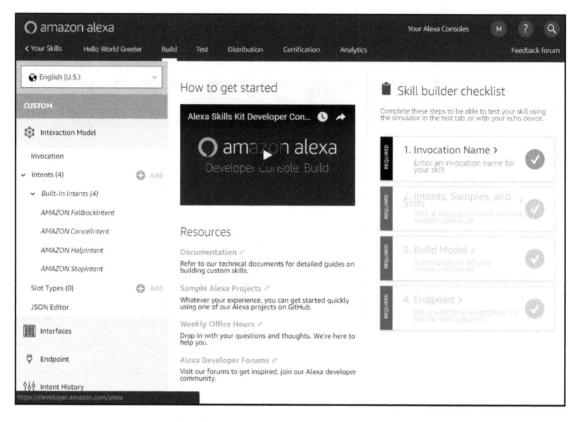

Figure 2.18: Completion of the first step (source: developer.amazon.com)

The first step should be completed now and marked as green. Now we will set up an intent for our skill.

7. Please click on the **Intents, Samples and Slots** button under the **Skill builder checklist**:

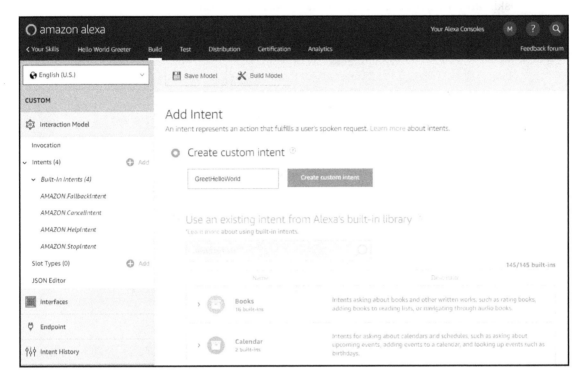

Figure 2.19: Creating the GreetHelloWorld intent (source: developer.amazon.com)

Please add the intent name as `GreetHelloWorld` and click on the **Create custom intent** button.

Although this is not immediately obvious, intents are defined in the JSON format as a part of the interaction model.

To find out more about the JSON format, please visit `https://www.json.org/`.

Our skill is comprised of a single intent: GreetHelloWorld. However, there are four other intents that are automatically defined by the **Alexa Skills Kit** for every skill and the overall intent schema looks like the following:

```json
{
    "interactionModel": {
        "languageModel": {
            "invocationName": "hello world greeter",
            "intents": [
                {
                    "name": "AMAZON.FallbackIntent",
                    "samples": []
                },
                {
                    "name": "AMAZON.CancelIntent",
                    "samples": []
                },
                {
                    "name": "AMAZON.HelpIntent",
                    "samples": []
                },
                {
                    "name": "AMAZON.StopIntent",
                    "samples": []
                },
                {
                    "name": "GreetHelloWorld",
                    "slots": [],
                    "samples": []
                }
            ],
            "types": []
        }
    }
}
```

If you are interested in knowing what ASK is doing under the hood, then you can see the preceding intent schema by clicking on the **JSON Editor** button.

8. Next, we define the **Sample Utterances** for the `GreetHelloWorld` intent, as shown in the following screenshot:

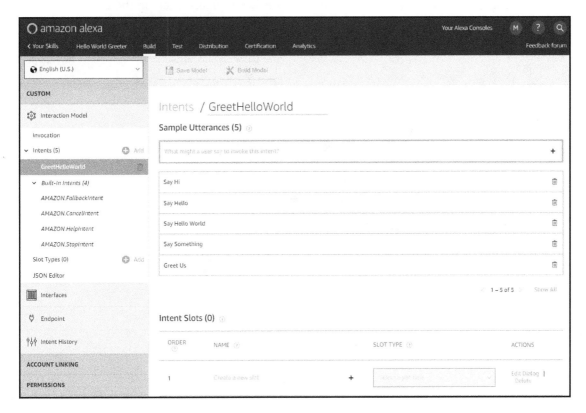

Figure 2.20: Sample utterances for the GreetHelloWorld intent (source: developer.amazon.com)

Please note that we are not defining any slots since this skill does not need any. We will look at the usage of slots in upcoming chapters.

Please click the **Save Model** button at the bottom of the screen to save these changes. Finally, please click on the **Build** tab to land on the **Skill builder checklist** again. On the **Skill builder checklist**, please click on the **Build Model** button:

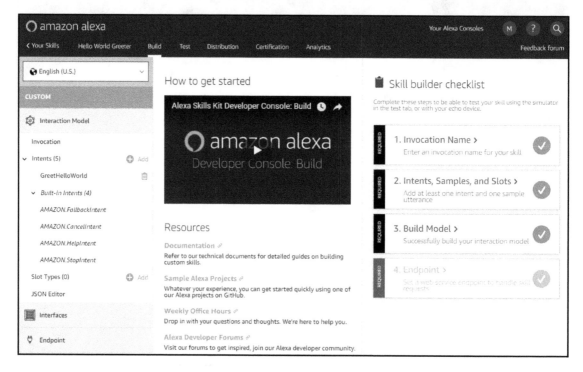

Figure 2.21: Building the interaction model (source: developer.amazon.com)

It will take a few seconds before the changes are saved and the actual interaction model is built/created. We will not move to the next step yet but configure our Lambda first. The reason for this will become evident in the coming steps.

9. Once the interaction model is created, we will leave the **Skill builder checklist** screen as is and will focus on creating the Lambda. However, before that, please click on the **Endpoint** button on the **Skill builder checklist** screen:

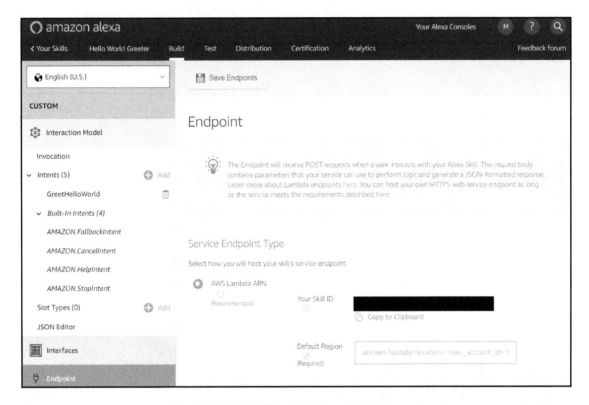

Figure 2.22: Copying the AWS Lambda ARN (source: developer.amazon.com)

Please select the AWS Lambda ARN and copy the skill ID and save it somewhere. We will need this skill ID in the coming steps.

10. Now, please open a new browser tab and navigate to the AWS console.

The AWS console can be found at `https://console.aws.amazon.com`. Please note that you will need to create a new account if you don't already have one.

Once you have navigated and successfully logged into the AWS console, you should see something similar to the following screenshot:

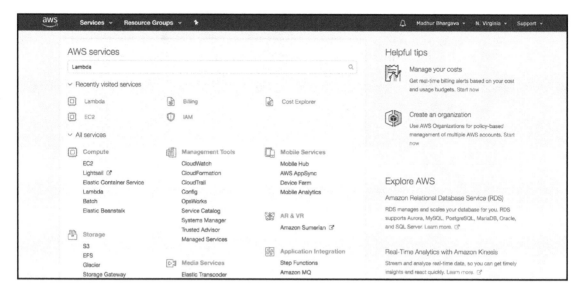

Figure 2.23: Searching for Lambda on the AWS services console (source: console.aws.amazon.com)

On the console search bar, please search for `Lambda`, and click on it when it appears in the list of auto-suggestions.

11. Select **Create a function** on the next screen:

Figure 2.24: AWS Lambda dashboard (source: console.aws.amazon.com)

12. On the next screen, you can either choose to author a Lambda from scratch or choose from one of the existing templates. We will choose to **Author from scratch** as this is our first skill and rather a simple one. Also, authoring from scratch gives us slightly greater insight into the code of the skill:

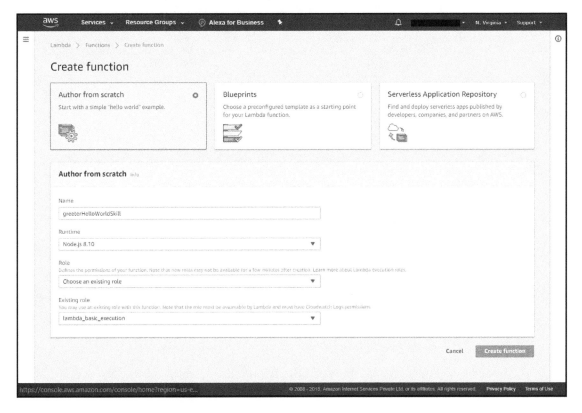

Figure 2.25: Authoring a Lambda function from scratch (source: console.aws.amazon.com)

As shown in the preceding screenshot, our Lambda function will be called greeterHelloWorldSkill, will use a Node.js(8.10) runtime, and will have an existing role of **lambda_basic_execution**. Please click **Create function** at the bottom of the screen after populating the necessary details.

13. Once the function has been created, you will be taken to the next screen, where you can add triggers. A trigger is a source that will activate our Lambda:

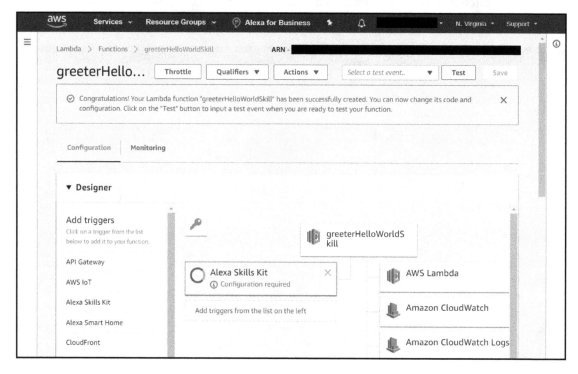

Figure 2.26: Adding the Alexa Skills Kit trigger to the Lambda (source: console.aws.amazon.com)

In our case, the trigger is **Alexa Skills Kit**. Please select this from the list of triggers on the left.

Please note that if you cannot find **Alexa Skills Kit** in the list of triggers on the left, make sure that you have selected the region as **North Virginia"(N. Virginia)** in the top left of the screen. This is because of the fact that, at the time of writing, only the North Virginia region hosts the **Alexa Skills Kit**.

With our trigger set, we will now need to configure it. Please copy the **Skill ID** that we saved in the previous step and add it to the skill verification section, as shown in the following screenshot:

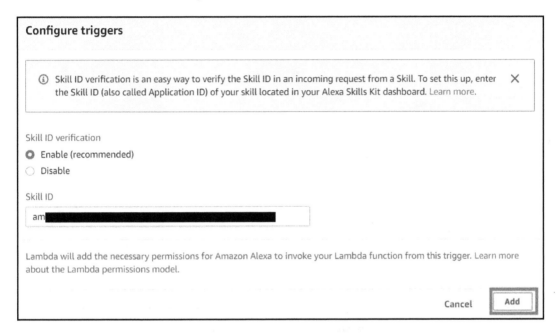

Figure 2.27: Adding the skill ID verification to the Lambda (source: console.aws.amazon.com)

The skill ID verification ensures that our Lambda handles only those queries that are sent by the skill we actually want to interact with.

Please click on the **Save** button at the top-right of the screen and select the **greeterHelloWorldSkill** under the designer tree:

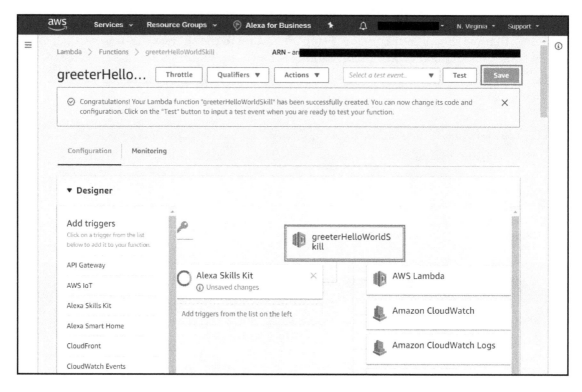

Figure 2.28: Configuring the Lambda (source: console.aws.amazon.com)

We can now configure and start writing the Lambda.

14. Since our skill is very simple, our Lambda will be handling two basic requests:
    - `LaunchRequest`: To handle the launch of a skill
    - `IntentRequest`: To handle various intents (in our case just one, `GreetHelloWorldIntent`, to greet Hello World)

We will be editing the code inline on the Developer portal itself. We will start by segregating each of the requests that our skill receives:

```
exports.handler = (event, context, callback) => {
    switch (event.request.type) {
        case "LaunchRequest":
            break;
        case "IntentRequest":
            break;
    }
}
```

As shown in the preceding code, this is how we segregate the launch and intent event requests.

15. Next, we will define some helper functions that will help us to create speech responses:

```
buildSpeechletResponse = (outputText, shouldEndSession) => {
  return {
    outputSpeech: {
      type: "PlainText",
      text: outputText
    },
    shouldEndSession: shouldEndSession
  }
}

generateResponse = (speechletResponse) => {
  return {
    version: "1.0",
    response: speechletResponse
  }
}
```

The generateResponse function will generate the response returned by the Lambda function using the buildSpeechletResponse function. The buildSpeechletResponse function will specify the output that Alexa will eventually speak, in the form of plain text. It also takes another variable, shouldEndSession, which specifies whether Alexa should end the session after the response or not.

16. Once we have the helper functions configured, we can update the LaunchRequest and IntentRequest cases to have Alexa say relevant responses, as shown in the following code:

```
exports.handler = (event, context, callback) => {
    switch (event.request.type) {
        case "LaunchRequest":
context.succeed(generateResponse(buildSpeechletResponse("Welcom
e to Hello World Greeter.", false)))
            break;
        case "IntentRequest":
            switch (event.request.intent.name) {
                case "GreetHelloWorld":
context.succeed(generateResponse(buildSpeechletResponse("Hello
World", true)))
                    break;
            }
            break;
    }
}
```

Now, when our Lambda receives a LaunchRequest, it can send a welcome message back, as shown in the preceding code. Also, if it receives an IntentRequest, it can filter down on an intent's name (although filtering is not needed currently since we have only one custom intent). Please save your progress by clicking **Save** at the top-right corner of the screen.

17. We need to link the Lambda to our skill and, to do this we will need the ARN of our Lambda.

ARN stands for Amazon Resource Number.

The ARN is located at the top-right corner of the Lambda function page, as shown in the following screenshot (the ARN in the image has been obfuscated for privacy and security reasons):

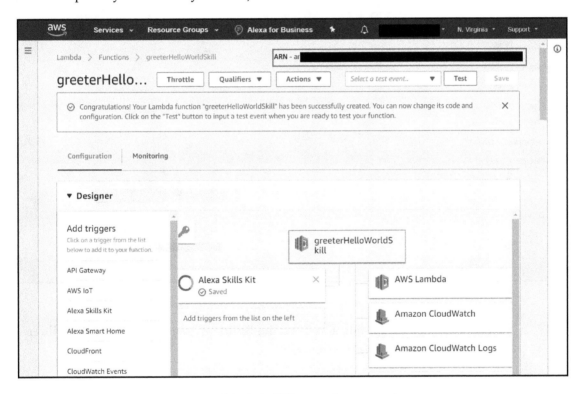

Figure 2.29: Copying the ARN (source: console.aws.amazon.com)

Once you have copied the ARN, please navigate to the previous browser tab, where we were configuring the interaction model of our skill. Please select the **Endpoints** tab and enter the ARN under **Default Region,** as shown in the following screenshot:

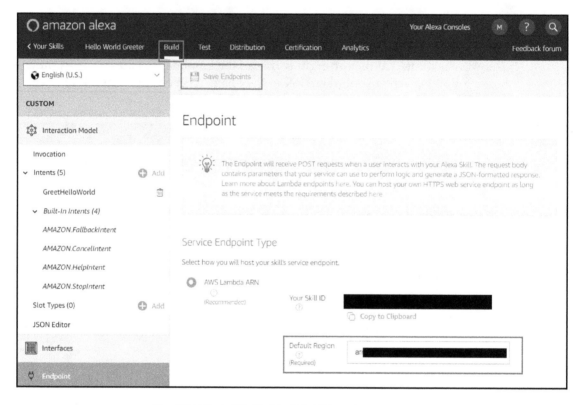

Figure 2.30: Linking the ARN of Lambda with the skill (source: developer.amazon.com)

Please click **Save Endpoints** and press the **Build** tab to land on the **Skill builder checklist**. Please build the model again.

18. Our setup is almost complete and we are ready to test our `Hello World Greeter` skill. The skill can be tested via the actual Amazon Echo device or via the Amazon Service Simulator. We will first test our skill via the Amazon Service Simulator. Please click on the **Test** tab to launch the Simulator and enable the test for the skill by flipping the **Test Switch**:

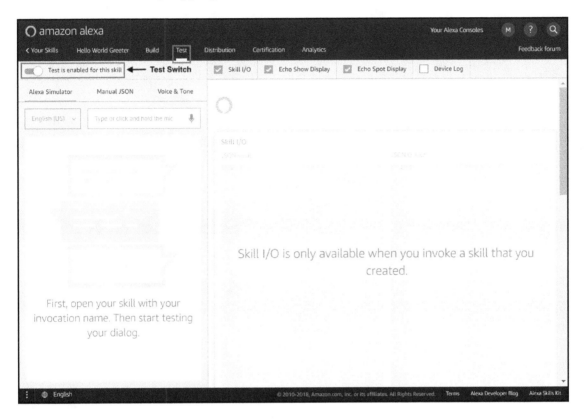

Figure 2.31: Alexa Test Simulator (source: developer.amazon.com)

Please enter the requests, as shown in the following screenshot. The Lambda should be invoked for each request and it should return the following responses:

Figure 2.32: Lambda responses in the Service Simulator (source: developer.amazon.com)

You can even listen to the responses if the volume of the system is turned on.

Alternatively, you can test the skill using Amazon Echo. Providing the Echo is connected and set up, if you utter: "Alexa, Launch Hello World Greeter," it should reply with "Welcome to Hello World Greeter." If you then ask it to "Say hi" or "Say something," it should reply "Hello World."

With this, we approach the end of this chapter.

 Please find the code for the Lambda for this chapter at the following link: https://github.com/madhurbhargava/AlexaSkillsProjects/blob/master/Chapter2_HelloWorldGreeter_index.js.

In the next section, we will summarize what we have learned and what can be expected from the upcoming chapters.

Summary

Please give yourself a pat on the back if you made it this far, having created the `Hello World Greeter` skill. Successful completion of this exercise proves that you just leveled up from being a novice to a Padawan. We still have a lot of skills to design before you can formally call yourself an Alexa Skills Jedi but we are off to a good start.

We hope that you now understand the anatomy of a basic Alexa Skill and the jargon surrounding it, such as Lambdas, intents, and slots. Also, you should now be able to design simple skills yourself.

In the coming chapters, we will gradually move on to slightly more complicated skills, each with an increasing level of difficulty as we proceed through each of the chapters. For example, in the next chapter, we will create an Alexa Skill that will enable us to use Alexa as a messaging medium, and from there we will move on to design other complex voice interfaces and skills, such as trivia games and smart home skills.

The future is voice!

3
Hands-Free Experience with Alexa

"The tongue can paint what the eyes can't see."

– Chinese Proverb

We moved on from learning about the details of Echo and Alexa to designing a basic Alexa Skill. We also gained some familiarity with the anatomy of a basic Alexa Skill and how the various moving parts in a skill interact with each other.

In this chapter, we take our design skills a little further and create a slightly more advanced skill. Our skill is called **Handsfree Messenger** and it will allow the user to leverage Alexa to send SMSes in a hands-free manner, just using Alexa and Echo, without any interaction with his/her phone. We will use a custom service called **Twilio**, which allows a user/developer to make/receive phone calls programmatically and send/receive text messages using web service APIs, in addition to AWS, where we will be hosting our Lambda.

We do this by covering the following topics in this chapter:

- Overview of the Handsfree Messenger Skill
- Configuring the Twilio Messaging Backend
- Configuring the Handsfree Messenger Skill

Without further ado, let's begin with an overview of the design of the skill.

Overview of the Handsfree Messenger Skill

Before we go ahead and design the Handsfree Messenger skill, we will need to understand a few things:

- What is the system's core functionality?
- What are all of its moving parts?
- How do these parts interact?

The Handsfree Messenger skill will work as follows:

1. The user will start the Alexa Skill by saying a start phrase—"Alexa, Start Handsfree Messenger."
2. Alexa will launch the skill.
3. The user will voice the actual message that needs to be sent: "Send message – Get milk!"
4. Now, this is where it gets interesting. When the user voices the actual message in the previous step, a `SendMessage` intent will be created and the actual message text will be passed as an argument to that intent.

 We have already discussed intents in the previous chapter and so we are assuming that the reader is already familiar with intents and their functionality.

5. The intent is processed by the Lambda, where the Lambda extracts the message from the intent and passes it to the Twilio backend, together with information about the intended recipient of the message.

 We will not go into many details about the communication between the Lambda and the Twilio backend since it will be covered in the upcoming sections.

6. The Twilio backend passes the received message to its intended recipient and passes a confirmation response to the Lambda.
7. The Lambda receives the confirmation and informs the sender by voicing the phrase `Message sent.`

As you would have already gathered from the description of the system's functionality, these are the major moving parts of our Handsfree Messenger skill:

- The actual Alexa Skill: Handsfree Messenger
- The skill's Lambda residing on the AWS backend
- The Twilio backend

If you were to compare this skill to the one that we created in the previous chapter, then this skill would be a slightly more complex one, just due to the fact that it has more moving parts.

The VUI flow of the Handsfree Messenger is as follows:

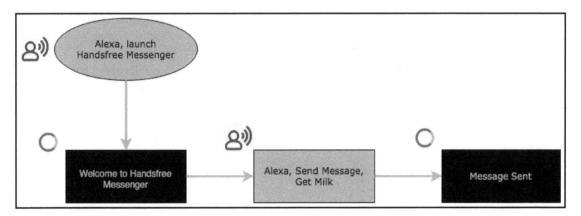

Figure 3.1: VUI flow for Handsfree Messenger

VUI flows are defined using an Amazon-preferred template to depict the VUI design of an Alexa Skill. However, VUI flows are limited to user interactions with Alexa, and so perhaps an overview of the functional steps as a diagram may help you understand the workings of the Handsfree Messenger skill better:

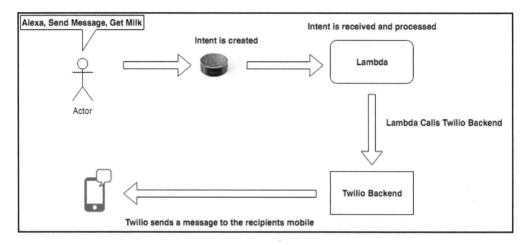

Figure 3.2: Functional steps for Handsfree Messenger skill

The preceding diagram outlines the basic use of the skill; we can also compress the steps into a flowchart to clarify the flow of information in the system:

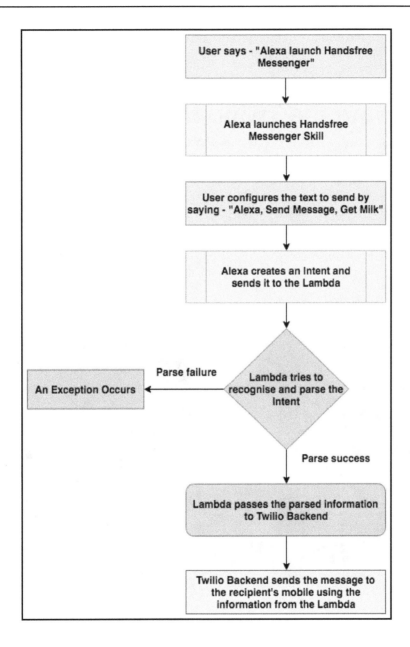

Figure 3.3: Information flow for HandsFree Messenger skill

We hope that it is now clear to the reader how our HandsFree Messenger skill will work and how all of its moving parts will interact.

In the next section, we will begin by configuring one of the moving parts, the Twilio backend for our skill.

Configuring the Twilio Messaging Backend

Twilio is a cloud communications platform that was founded in 2007 and is based in San Francisco. It allows a user/developer to make/receive phone calls programmatically and send/receive text messages using web service APIs. For this chapter, we shall only be demonstrating its messaging function; however, we request and anticipate that the reader will extend the functionality of this skill by adding the phone call functionality as a homework exercise.

To configure Twilio as our messaging backend, we shall be following these steps:

1. Please navigate to `www.twilio.com` in your web browser, as seen in this screenshot:

Fig 3.4: Twilio landing page

2. Please click on **Get a free API key** or **Sign up** (both will start the sign-up process for a new user) to land on the **Sign up for free** page shown here:

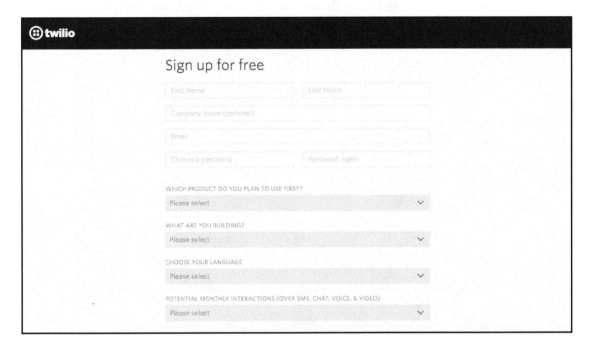

Figure 3.5: Twilio sign-up page

3. Please fill in your personal details. As shown in the previous screenshot, there is a small questionnaire towards the bottom of the page, which is built around use of the Twilio service. Please choose the following details for that questionnaire:

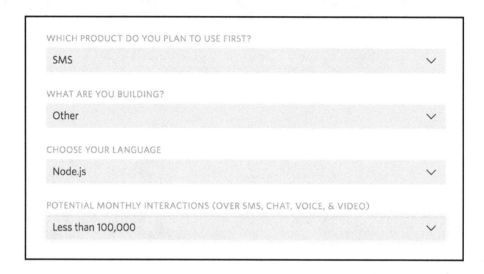

Figure 3.6: Twilio - Filling in personal details while registering

4. After you have filled in the details, please select the **Get Started** button located toward the bottom of the page. This should land you on this verification page:

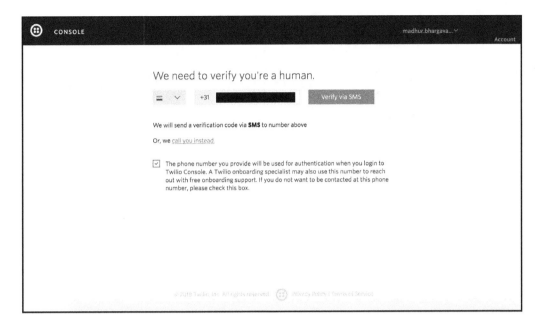

Figure 3.7: Twilio - verification process

Please select the appropriate country and enter your phone number in the space provided, then click on **Verify via SMS**, after which you should receive an SMS with a verification code on the phone number that you supplied.

5. Clicking on **Verify via SMS** should bring you to the next screen, where you can enter the verification code:

Figure 3.8: Twilio - verification process

Please enter the verification code on this screen and click on **Submit**.

6. If you were able to verify the SMS code successfully, then you should be presented with the project details screen where we will provide our project with a name, as shown here:

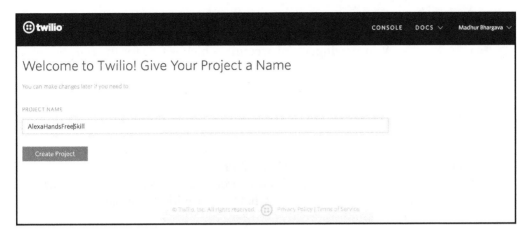

Figure 3.9: Twilio - Naming your Project

Please name the skill `AlexaHandsFreeSkill` and click on **Create Project**.

7. Clicking on the **Create Project** button should land us on this dashboard:

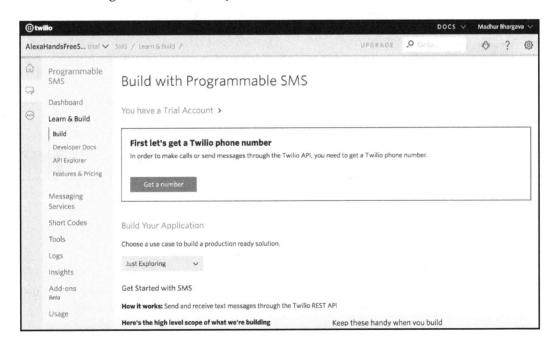

Figure 3.10: Twilio – Dashboard

There are a few things that are noticeable on the dashboard:

- We are using a trial account, which is fine for the purpose of this skill.
- We need to get a Twilio number.

Firstly, let's try to understand why we need a Twilio number.

The way Twilio works is as follows—a developer initially requests a Twilio number, and when they use the Twilio API to send SMSes or make calls, those SMSes and calls are generated from this prerequested number. Each generated Twilio number is tied to the country that you provided as a part of your details in Step 2 and its communication laws.

8. Please click on the **Get a number** button on the dashboard screen shown in Step 7. This should generate a phone number, depending on the country details that you supplied in Step 2:

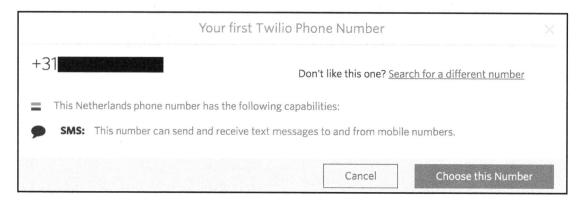

Figure 3.11: Getting a Twilio number

Our skill will be making use of the generated number for sending SMSes via Twilio API calls.

9. When you select **Choose this Number** in the Twilio phone number dialog, which is presented to the user in the previous step, depending on the country, the user may be asked for additional details as shown in the following screenshot:

Address Required   ×

Due to local regulation, you or your customer must have a business or personal address from any country to purchase +31 ▮▮▮▮▮▮▮▮

Enter an Address

FRIENDLY NAME	name for the address
CUSTOMER NAME	name for business or customer
ADDRESS 1	Street address, PO box, suit, unit, etc.
ADDRESS 2	Additional street address, PO box, suit, unit, etc.
CITY	
STATE/PROVINCE/REGION	
POSTAL CODE	
COUNTRY	☰ Netherlands ∨

❮ Go back to your preselected number   Cancel   Save and continue

Figure 3.12: Twilio: Address requirement for the number

Please note that the dialog box shown here is dependent on the country that the user selected as a part of the onboarding process, and depending on the country, you may or may not see this dialog. If you are presented with this dialog, then please provide the necessary details and click the **Save and continue** button toward the bottom of the dialog.

10. On clicking the **Save and continue** button, we should be presented with this dialog box:

Fig 3.13: Finally getting the Twilio number

The number selection process is finalized and we have now successfully selected a phone number to send SMSes via Twilio API calls. Please click on the **Done** button in this dialog box, and you should end up at the dashboard again.

11. Once you end up at the dashboard, toward the bottom there should be a **Get Started** with SMS section with a **Get Started** button:

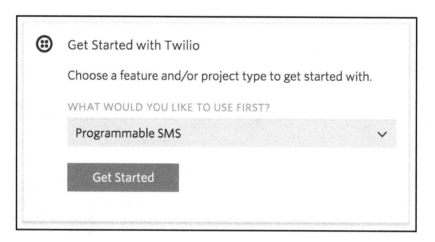

Figure 3.14: Twilio - Getting started with Programmable SMS

Under this section, please select **Programmable SMS** from the dropdown and click on the **Get Started** button.

12. On clicking the **Get Started** button, you should end up on the **Send a Message** page:

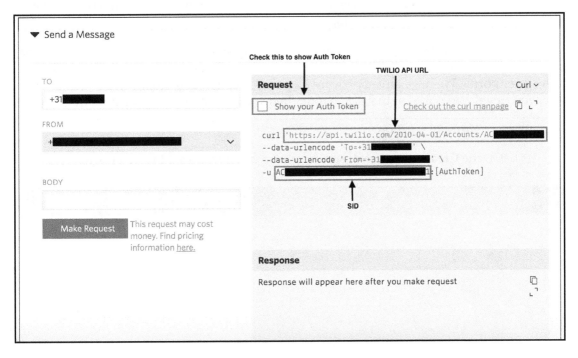

Figure 3.15: Twilio - Test setup for sending a message functionality

Please note that we need three important pieces of information from this page:

- **SID**: Marked in the previous screenshot
- **Auth Token**: If you check the box marked **Show your Auth Token**, the Auth Token will become visible
- **Twilio API URL**: This is mentioned following the `curl` command

Please note down the SID and the Auth Token as we will be needing those in the Lambda code. After you have noted these details down, please dismiss this page.

We have successfully configured the Twilio backend, which will help us send SMSes using our Alexa Skill. In the next section, we will configure our Handsfree Messenger skill via the Amazon Developer console.

Configuring the Handsfree Messenger Skill

With our Twilio backend in place, we now need to configure the Alexa Skill. For this, we will configure via the Amazon Developer portal.

We will assume that the reader knows and has already signed up to the Amazon Developer portal, and is already aware of basic starter information about the Amazon Alexa Skills Developer portal. We have already covered account creation and other basic details for the Amazon Developer portal in the last chapter, hence we would not be repeating those here.

We will start with skill creation:

1. On the **Create a new skill** screen, please provide the skill with a name:

Figure 3.16: Creating the Handsfree Messenger skill

Please save these changes and move on to the next screen by using the **Next** button at the top right of the screen.

2. In this step, we shall choose a model for our skill.

We have already covered the specifics of choosing a model in `Chapter 2`, *Hello World, Alexa!*, so we won't be going into much detail here. Please select a **Custom** model for the skill and move on to the next screen, the Skill builder checklist, after creating the Skill.

We already know from `Chapter 2`, *Hello World, Alexa!*, that an interaction model consists of intents, slots, and sample utterances. The interaction model of the Handsfree Messenger skill consists of all of those, which we will define in the following steps by completing the **Skill builder checklist**.

3. As the first step in the **Skill builder checklist**, we will provide an **Invocation Name** for our skill. The **Invocation Name** for our skill will be `handsfree messenger`. This is the name that users use to invoke our skill. Please save the model after providing the invocation name.

4. Next, we will need to configure an intent for our skill. Our skill consists of a single intent, `SendMessage`. We define the intent as follows:

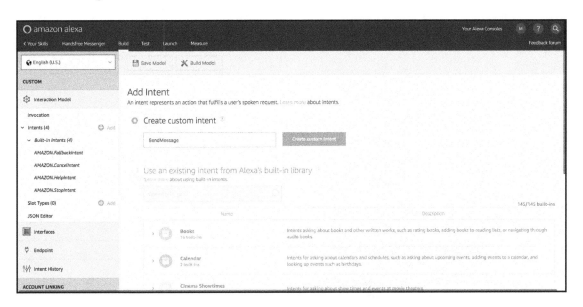

Figure 3.17: Creating the SendMessage intent

Please click on the **Create custom intent** button to create the intent.

But that is not all; we will also need to include a slot in the intent schema so that we can pass the message text as an argument to the Lambda.

Slot: Simply stated, a slot contains the extra pieces of data that can be passed with an intent. In our case, we will be defining a custom slot type, which we use to pass message text with the `SendMessage` intent.

We will include a custom slot type in our intent schema in the next step, which will hold the text for the SMS.

5. Once the intent is created, please scroll down the intent details screen and add a custom slot with the name `Text`. Add the slot and provide it with a predefined type of **AMAZON.SearchQuery** from the dropdown as shown in the following screenshot:

Figure 3.18: Alexa Skill – Adding a custom slot to a skill

We have included a custom slot with the name `Text` and type **AMAZON.SearchQuery**.

 Although a confusing name, the **AMAZON.SearchQuery** slot type can be used to pass any type of phrase to your Lambda by containing it in a slot.

This slot will hold the message text to be passed as an argument to the `SendMessage` intent.

To know more about slots, types, and custom slot types, please visit
https://developer.amazon.com/docs/custom-skills/custom-
interaction-model-reference.html#custom-slot-syntax.

6. Next up, we will need to define some sample utterances for the Handsfree
Messenger skill, which will, in turn, launch the `SendMessage` intent:

Figure 3.19: Specifying sample utterances for a skill

If you notice, in the sample utterances shown, all of them contain a custom slot
type, `{Text}`, which will contain the spoken message/phrase.

Please click the **Save Model** button at the top left of the screen to save these
changes.

We will not move to the next step yet and configure our Lambda first. However, before
that, please copy our skill ID from the **Endpoints** section under the **Skill builder checklist**
and save it somewhere. We will need it in the next section to link it with the Lambda for
skill ID validation. Since we have also performed this step in `Chapter 2`, *Hello World, Alexa!*,
we are not repeating the details here.

Coding the Lambda function

Once the interaction model has been created, we will leave this screen as is and will focus on creating the Lambda.

1. Please open a new browser tab and navigate to AWS console, the web URL for which is mentioned here:

 The AWS console can be found at `https://console.aws.amazon.com`. Please note that you may need to create a new account if not already created.

We have already covered the creation of a basic Lambda function in Steps *8-12* in `Chapter 2`, *Hello World, Alexa!*, under the heading *Hello Alexa – Building a Hello World Alexa Skill*, so we shall not be repeating the steps here. Please follow those steps, name the Lambda function `handsFreeMesssengerSkill`, and link the skill ID with the Lambda, as previously described in `Chapter 2`, *Hello World, Alexa!* under the heading *Hello Alexa – Building a Hello World Alexa Skill*.

Since our skill is very simple, our Lambda will be handling two basic requests:

*   **Launch request**: To handle launching the skill
*   **Intent request**: To handle various Intents (in our case, just one, `SendMessage`, to send the actual SMS)

We will be editing the code inline, in the `index.js` file in the developer portal itself. We shall start by segregating each of the requests that our Skill receives. For this, please declare the following handler:

```
exports.handler = function (event, context) {
    try {

        if (event.request.type === "LaunchRequest") {
        } else if (event.request.type === "IntentRequest") {
        }
    } catch (e) {
        context.fail("Exception: " + e);
    }
};
```

This is how we segregate the launch and intent event requests.

2. Next up, we will define some helper functions that will help us in creating speech responses:

```
//-------Helper Methods---------//

function buildSpeechletResponse(output, shouldEndSession) {
    return {
        outputSpeech: {
            type: "PlainText",
            text: output
        },
        shouldEndSession: shouldEndSession
    };
}

function buildResponse(speechletResponse) {
    return {
        version: "1.0",
        response: speechletResponse
    };
}
```

These functions help the Lambda to return the response to be spoken by Alexa whenever it receives a specific intent/input.

The `buildResponse` function will generate the plainspoken response which shall eventually be voiced by Alexa.

The `buildSpeechletResponse` function will specify the output that Alexa will eventually speak, in the form of plain text. It also takes another variable, `shouldEndSession`, which specifies whether Alexa should end the session after the response or not.

3. Once we have the helper functions configured, we can update the handling of `LaunchRequest` and `IntentRequest` cases to have Alexa speak with relevant responses, as shown here:

```
exports.handler = function (event, context) {
    try {
        if (event.request.type === "LaunchRequest") {
            onLaunch(function callback(speechletResponse) {
context.succeed(buildResponse(speechletResponse));
                });
        } else if (event.request.type === "IntentRequest") {
            onIntent(event.request,
                function callback(speechletResponse) {
```

```
                    context.succeed(buildResponse(speechletResponse));
                                    });
                }
            } catch (e) {
                context.fail("Exception: " + e);
            }
        };
```

Now, when our Lambda receives a `LaunchRequest`, it will call the `onLaunch` method to send a welcome message back, which we will implement in the next step.

Also, if it receives an `IntentRequest`, it can call the `onIntent` method, which in turn will filter down on the intent's name (although filtering is not needed currently since we have only one custom intent).

Save your progress by clicking **Save** in the top-right corner of the screen.

4. We shall now implement the `onLaunch` and the `onIntent` methods that we discussed in the previous step:

```
function onLaunch(callback) {
    var output = "Welcome to HandsFree Messenger.";
    var endSession = false;
    callback(buildSpeechletResponse(output, endSession));
}

function onIntent(intentRequest, callback) {
    var intent = intentRequest.intent,
        intentName = intentRequest.intent.name;
    if("SendMessage" === intentName){
        var text = intent.slots.Text.value;
        var recipient = '+31XXXXXXXXXX';
        SendMessage(recipient, text,callback);
    } else {
        throw "Intent not recognized";
    }
}
```

The `onLaunch` method is simple—it creates a welcome message and sends it back after creating a speech response out of that message, using the helper methods we defined earlier.

The `onIntent` method is comparatively tricky—it filters out the intent based on its name and if the intent is the `SendMessage` intent, then it extracts the SMS text from the slot value before forwarding it to the recipient's hard-coded mobile number via the `SendMessage` function.

We shall define the `SendMessage` function in the coming steps.

5. The `SendMessage` function is the juice of the whole skill. It is the one responsible for passing the message to the Twilio backend. However, before defining the `SendMessage` function, we need to declare a few constants that will be required while interacting with the Twilio API.

   If you remember, we noted down the SID and the Auth Token in the last step of the previous section; it is time now to declare them. We will be using these constants in the `SendMessage` function. Declare those variables as shown here:

   ```
   var sid = 'ACXXXXXXXXXXXXXXXXXXXXXXXXXXXXXXXX';
   var token = '4bXXXXXXXXXXXXXXXXXXXXXXXXXXXXXXXX';
   var sender = '+31XXXXXXXXXX';

   var https = require('https');
   var queryString = require('querystring');
   ```

Define these constants at the very top of the `index.js` file on the AWS developer portal. After defining them, the `index.js` file on the developer portal should resemble the one shown here:

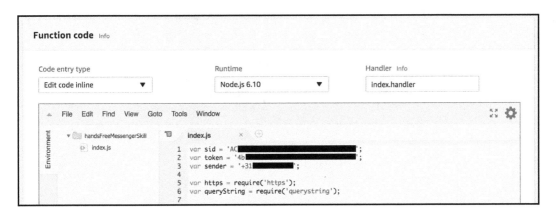

Figure 3.20: Coding the Lambda

Please note that we have declared the same Twilio number as the `sender` that we generated in Step *11* in the previous section.

6. With our constants ready, we can now finally define the `SendMessage` function:

```
function SendMessage(to, body, callback) {
    var message = {
        To: to,
        From: sender,
        Body: body
    };
    var messageString = queryString.stringify(message);
    var options = {
        host: 'api.twilio.com',
        port: 443,
        path: '/2010-04-01/Accounts/' + sid + '/Messages.json',
        method: 'POST',
        headers: {
                    'Content-Type': 'application/x-www-form-
urlencoded',
                    'Content-Length':
Buffer.byteLength(messageString),
                    'Authorization': 'Basic ' + new Buffer(sid
+ ':' + token).toString('base64')
                }
    };
    var req = https.request(options, function (res) {
        res.setEncoding('utf-8');
        var responseString = '';
        res.on('data', function (data) {
            responseString += data;
        });
        res.on('end', function () {
      var speechOutput = "Message sent.";
      var shouldEndSession = true;
      callback(buildSpeechletResponse(speechOutput,
shouldEndSession));
        });
    });
    req.write(messageString);
    req.end();
}
```

There is a lot going on in this function. The `SendMessage` function constructs a message object, which contains information about the sender, the recipient, and the text to send.

It then places a request to the Twilio backend with the `SID`, `AuthToken`, and `message string` as parameters.

The successful sending of the message is marked by Alexa confirming it by saying the phrase, "Message sent."

After you have added this code, please save your progress by clicking **Save** in the top-right corner of the screen.

7. Now, we need to link the Lambda to our skill and for this purpose, we will need the **Amazon Resource Number** (**ARN**) of our Lambda. The ARN is located in the top-right corner of the Lambda function/Code Editor page. Please copy the ARN and once you have copied it, please navigate to the previous browser tab, where we were configuring the interaction model of our skill using the **Skill builder checklist**. Please select the **Endpoint** section from the Skill builder checklist to land on the **Endpoint** screen:

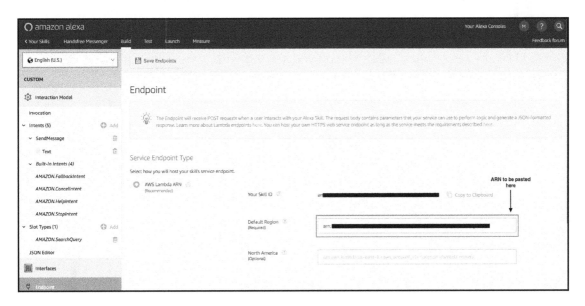

Figure 3.21: Configuring the skill

Please select **AWS Lambda ARN** as **Service Endpoint Type** and enter the ARN that we copied earlier (obfuscated in the preceding screenshot for privacy and security reasons), leave the other options on this screen as is and click the **Save Endpoints** button.

Please navigate back to the **Skill builder checklist** and build the interaction model.

Testing the Skill

Our setup is almost complete and we are ready to test our Handsfree Messenger skill. The skill can be tested via the actual Amazon Echo device or via the Alexa Simulator.

Since we have already used the Alexa Simulator in Chapter 2, *Hello World, Alexa!*, this time you can test the skill using an actual Amazon Echo, provided you have one and the Echo is connected and set up. Then, if you say "Alexa, launch Handsfree Messenger," it should reply with "Welcome to Handsfree Messenger." If you then say, "Send message – Pick up groceries," it should reply "Message sent" and an SMS with the text "Pick up groceries" should be delivered to the recipient.

Please note that each free Twilio account comes with a small balance and, hence, sending a few messages (10-20) will not incur any cost to you.

Our skill is now tested and ready to be played around with. You can find the code for the Lambda from this chapter at the link mentioned in the information box.

Please find the code for the Lambda at the following URL https://github.com/madhurbhargava/AlexaSkillsProjects/blob/master/Chapter3_HandsFreeMessenger_index.js.

With this, we have reached the end of this chapter.

Summary

We do hope you enjoyed creating the Handsfree Messenger skill, which was slightly more evolved than our previous skill and oriented toward the practical use of Alexa/Echo devices. The skill that we created in this section still has room for a lot of improvement. For example, currently, our skill sends messages to predefined/hard-coded recipients, which can be improved by passing the recipient details via a slot to the Lambda so that it does not have to be predefined in the Lambda. We intentionally did not cover this and it is intended to be an extension exercise, which we highly recommend that you undertake if you really want to be an Alexa Skills Jedi sooner.

But, we again completed one more interesting Alexa Skill.

In the next chapter, we will extend our faculties regarding Alexa knowledge a little further by creating an Alexa Skill that is more oriented towards entertainment, will use a slightly more complex voice interface, and will be even more fun.

Can't wait to get started? Let's begin!

4
Let's Play Factly with Alexa

"The human voice is the most perfect instrument of all."

– Arvo Part

We have been making progress by leaps and bounds in our quest to become an Alexa Skills Jedi. We started by designing a Hello World Alexa Skill, which made us understand the finer details of a basic Alexa Skill. Armed with that knowledge, we continued to expand our arsenal by developing a slightly more advanced Alexa Skill, which also communicated with a third-party backend (Twilio).

In this chapter, we will take a slight detour and create a self-contained skill called **Factly**. Factly will be a trivia/quiz-oriented Alexa Skill that can quiz a user regarding various facts. It will be a self-contained skill and will *not* be communicating to any third-party APIs/backends.

We shall do this by covering the following topics in this chapter:

- Motivation for Designing Factly
- Designing the Factly Skill
- Building the Factly Skill

Without much further ado, let's begin with an overview of the design of the Skill.

Motivation for Designing Factly

Before we dive deep into the details of the Factly Alexa Skill, let's try to understand the reason for our choice of creating this Skill by understanding what people use voice assistants for.

In a study done by Statista on smartphone users in the UK, it was revealed that people who use voice assistants use them mainly for **Amusement**, which is second only to **Search for general information**, as shown in the following diagram:

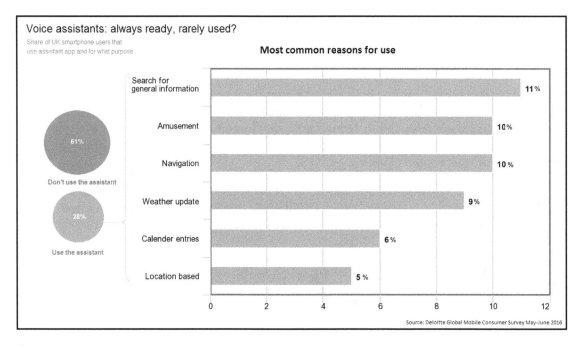

Figure 4.1: Most common uses of voice assistants

With this insight, it is no surprise also that the lion's share of Alexa Skills on the Amazon Alexa App Store belongs to games and trivia apps:

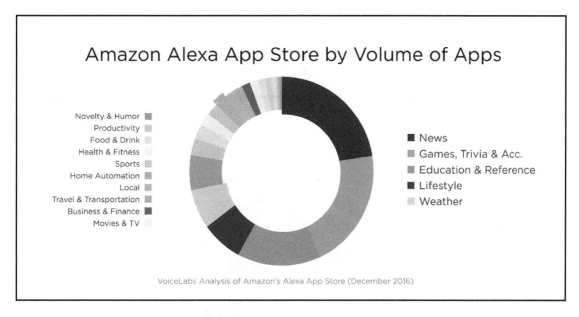

Figure 4.2: Alexa Skills categorisation on Amazon Alexa App Store

Surprisingly or unsurprisingly, this is very similar to the distribution of apps in the smartphone market:

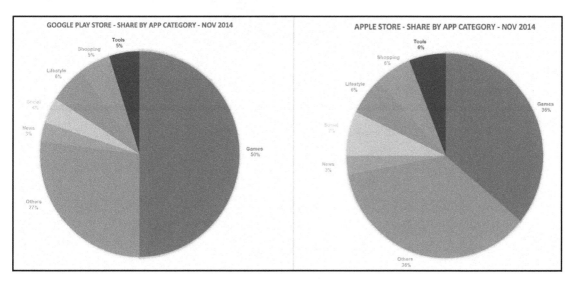

Figure 4.3: App domain dominance on Google Play and Apple's App Store

The majority of apps published are games, for both the Android and iOS platforms.

Users spent the most time on apps that fall into the category of **Gaming** and **Entertainment**, as shown in the following chart:

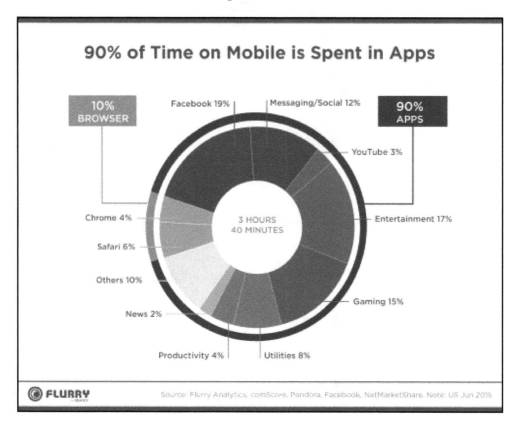

Figure 4.4: Time spent by an average mobile user in individual apps (source: Flurry)

A typical consumer spends 32% of their mobile phone time on **Entertainment/Gaming** apps.

We do not have such similarly insightful statistics yet for the Skills market since it is still in its nascent stages. However, we can make some fairly accurate decisions using what we can learn from the distribution of apps in the smartphone market, given that the number of Alexa Skills has grown quite rapidly from 2015 to 2017, as shown in the following chart:

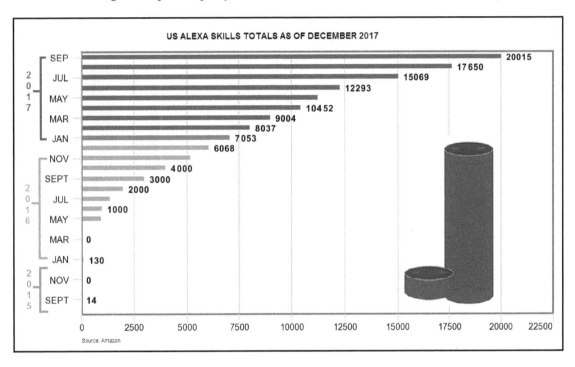

Fig 4.5: Growth of Alexa Skills market (source: voicebot.ai)

As shown above, as of September 2017, the total number of Alexa Skills in the US market alone stands roughly at 20,000, out of which at least 25% of the skills are games, trivia, and entertainment-oriented, that is, a ballpark figure of around 6,000, which is trivial when compared to the number of apps in the global smartphone market:

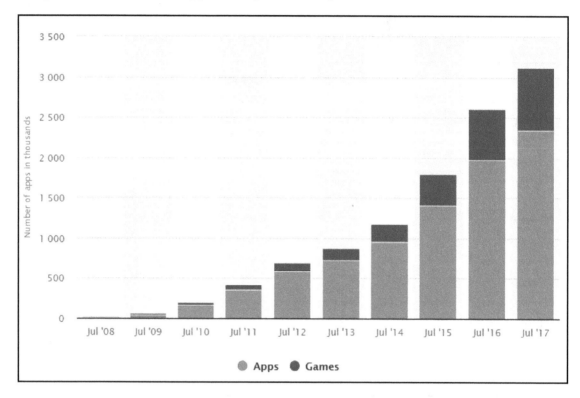

Figure 4.6: Number of available apps in Apple App Store over a time period (Data source: Apple)

The number of apps in the Apple App Store grew from 0 to 1.5 million over a period of 7 years and is still growing. Anticipating a similar trajectory and considering even a conservative growth rate, we can clearly hope for a similar growth in the voice skills market.

The preceding analysis brings us to the following conclusions:

- **Games/Entertainment** skills are and will always be the most downloaded and used skills, irrespective of the platform they are being developed for
- Compared to the smartphone apps market, the skills market is still in its infancy and there is a lot of room to grow

With the current count of **Games/Trivia**-oriented skills in the Alexa Skills store being around 6,000, there is a lot more room to accommodate other **Games/Trivia** skills, which is one of the major reasons that we decided to introduce our readers to the Factly Skill in this chapter.

Designing the Factly Skill

We hope that the discussion in the last section should have given you a fair idea of the motivation behind the Factly Alexa Skill. Now, we shall level up and design the actual Factly Skill. It is always better to design before coding anything because it gives us a clarity about the end goals of the software and the finer details, which we may otherwise miss when we actually code the software.

The Factly Alexa Skill is a simple quiz skill. At the code level, the Factly Skill/Lambda will contain a bank of questions that will be presented to the user one by one. The skill will further perform depending on the user's reply.

Factly will work via the following steps:

1. The user will launch the Factly Skill via a standard Alexa Skill launch utterance.
2. Alexa will confirm the launch and provide a brief introduction to the skill and play method:

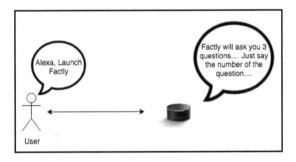

Figure 4.7: Step 1 – Factly, launch

The skill that we will design will consist of three trivia questions and each question will have four answer choices, with only a single choice being the correct one.

3. Alexa will begin the quiz by asking the first question:

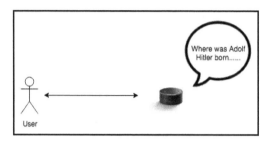

Figure 4.8: Step 2 – Factly, questionnaire

4. The user can provide the answer by just saying the number of the correct answer, for example: "The answer is 3" or just "3":

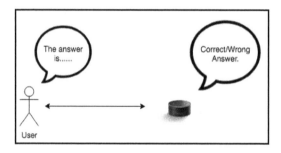

Figure 4.9: Step 3 – Factly, answer acknowledgment

Depending on the user's answer, the skill will provide a response that the answer is correct or incorrect.

5. The user can also end the session:

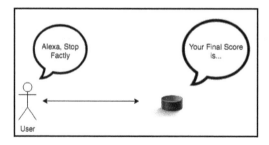

Figure 4.10: Step 4 – Factly, conclusion

6. Steps *4*, *5*, and *6* will be repeated until all the quiz questions have been exhausted or the user decides to end the session.

The interaction flow can be expressed in terms of a VUI diagram:

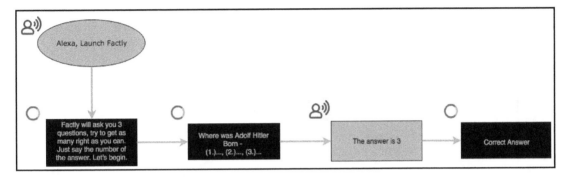

Figure 4.11: Factly, VUI flow

Also, the overall information flow of a typical quiz session can be mapped out as follows:

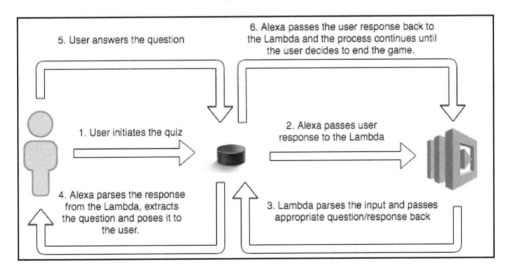

Figure 4.12: Factly, data flow

Also, we can map out the flow of data in the skill as per the following diagram:

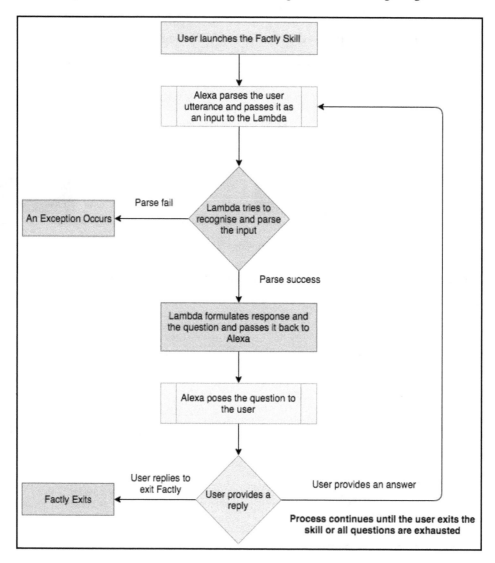

Figure 4.13: Factly, information flow

With our data flow in place, now it is time to code the actual Factly Skill.

Building the Factly Skill

Now, since we understand how data flows to and from our Factly Skill, it is time to actually build it. For this purpose, we will build the actual Lambda via the Amazon Developer portal.

We will assume that the reader knows about and has already signed up to the Amazon Developer portal, and is already aware of the basic starter information about the Amazon Alexa Skills Developer Portal, since this has also been already covered in detail in `Chapter 2`, *Hello World, Alexa!*. We already covered account creation and other basic details for the Amazon Developer Portal in `Chapter 2`, *Hello World, Alexa!*, so we will not be repeating those here.

We shall begin with the skill creation:

1. On the **Skill builder checklist**, select **Invocation Name** to navigate to the **Invocation** name screen and provide the skill with an invocation name, as shown in the following screenshot:

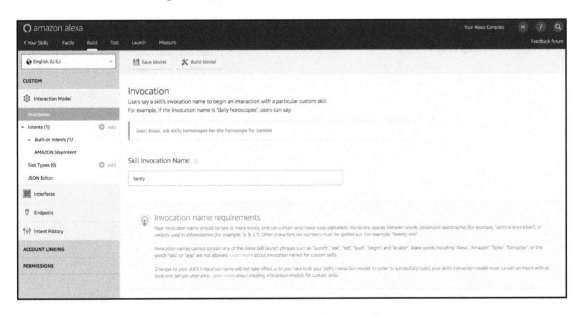

Figure 4.14: Alexa Skills dashboard – Adding Invocation Name

Save these changes by clicking on the **Save Model** button. Once you have successfully saved the changes, navigate back to the **Skill builder checklist**.

2. In this step, we shall define the **Intents, Samples, and Slots** for the **Interaction Model** for our skill. Our skill will be making use of two intents:

- **Answer Intent**: This intent will hold the user's answers to the quiz questions posed by the Factly Skill. This intent will also include a slot so that we can pass the answer as an argument to the Lambda.
- **AMAZON.StopIntent**: This is a standard intent pre-provided by ASK, through which the user can terminate the skill's execution at any point in time.

 To know more about standard built-in intents, please visit `https://developer.amazon.com/docs/custom-skills/standard-built-in-intents.html`.

From the **Skill builder checklist**, click on **Intents, Samples, and Slots** to land on the **Add Intent** screen. Rather than directly defining an Intent, we will first define a custom slot that we can later include in our **Answer Intent**:

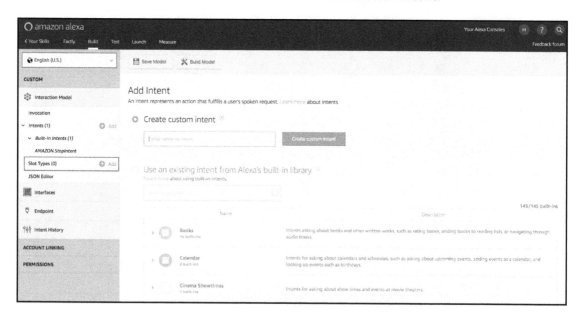

Figure 4.15: Adding a New Slot Type

As shown in the preceding screenshot, click on the **Add** button next to **Slot Types** to land on the **Add Slot Type** screen.

To know more about slots, types, and custom slot types, please visit https://developer.amazon.com/docs/custom-skills/custom-interaction-model-reference.html#custom-slot-syntax.

On the **Add Slot Type** screen, create a custom slot type by the name of LIST_OF_CHOICES, as shown in the following screenshot:

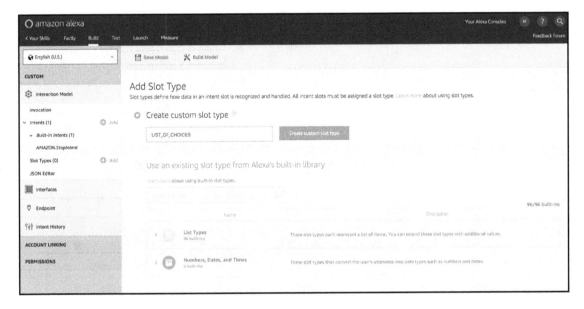

Figure 4.16: Naming the new custom Slot Type

On the next screen, provide it with a list of values, 1, 2, 3, 4, since each of the questions posed by the Factly Skill can have these four possible answers:

Figure 4.17: Adding Slot Values to the custom Slot Type

With our slot type set up, click on the **Add** button to add an intent, as shown in the following screenshot:

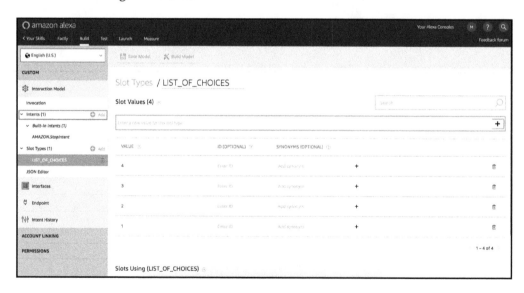

Figure 4.18: Adding an Intent

This should bring you to the **Add Intent** screen. Define an intent called `Answer` on this screen, which is going to contain the answer provided by the user for the questions posed by the Factly Skill, as shown in the following screenshot:

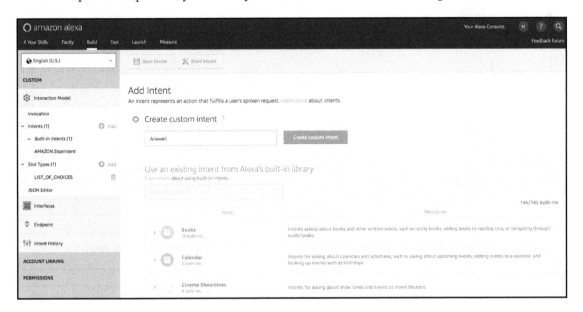

Figure 4.19: Naming the Intent

Once you have defined the intent, click on the **Create custom intent** button to land on the **Sample Utterances** screen. Before defining any sample utterances, scroll down on this screen and create a new slot type called `Choice`. Give this slot the type of `LIST_OF_CHOICES`, which we defined earlier from the drop-down menu:

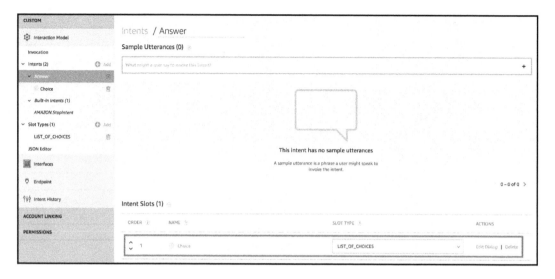

Figure 4.20: Adding slot to the Intent

Once we have defined the slot, we can now go ahead and define a couple of sample utterances for our intent.

3. Add a couple of **Sample Utterances** for the Answer intent which will, of course, include the **Choice** slot, since that is what will contain the actual answer to the questions posed by Factly:

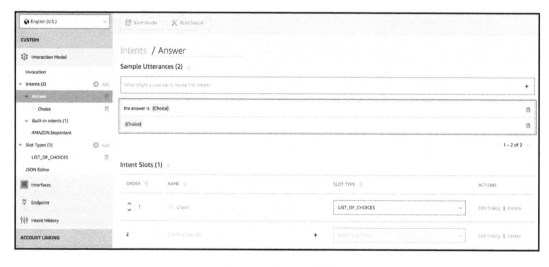

Figure 4.21: Adding Sample Utterances for the Intent

Once you have defined and saved the model, you can also click on the **JSON Editor** option in the left menu pane and verify that your JSON configuration matches this one:

```json
{
    "interactionModel": {
        "languageModel": {
            "invocationName": "factly",
            "intents": [
                {
                    "name": "Answer",
                    "slots": [
                        {
                            "name": "Choice",
                            "type": "LIST_OF_CHOICES"
                        }
                    ],
                    "samples": [
                        "the answer is {Choice}",
                        "{Choice}"
                    ]
                },
                {
                    "name": "AMAZON.StopIntent",
                    "samples": []
                }
            ],
            "types": [
                {
                    "name": "LIST_OF_CHOICES",
                    "values": [
                        {
                            "name": {
                                "value": "1"
                            }
                        },
                        {
                            "name": {
                                "value": "2"
                            }
                        },
                        {
                            "name": {
                                "value": "3"
                            }
                        },
                        {
```

```
                                        "name": {
                                            "value": "4"
                                        }
                                    }
                                ]
                            }
                        ]
                    }
                }
            }
```

After confirming the JSON configuration, navigate back to the **Skill builder checklist**.

4. From the **Skill builder checklist**, navigate to the **Endpoint** screen, copy the skill ID from the Endpoint screen, and save it somewhere. We will be needing it shortly.

Configuring the Lambda function

Once the **Interaction Model** is created, we will leave the configuration screen as it is for now and we will focus on creating the Lambda:

1. Open a new browser tab and navigate to the AWS Console, the web URL for which is mentioned in the following information box:

The AWS console can be found at `https://console.aws.amazon.com`. Please note that you may need to create a new account if one is not already created.

Name the Lambda function `factlySkill` and fill in the details as shown in the following screenshot:

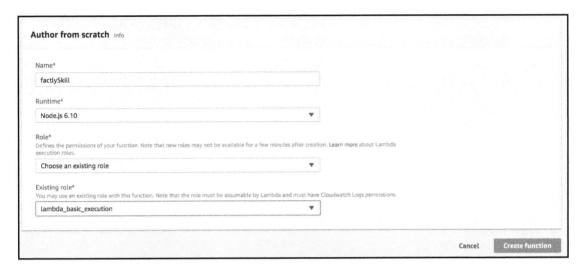

Figure 4.22: Naming the Lambda

Click on the **Create function** button after filling in the details.

2. On the next screen, under the **Designer** section, you will need to add a trigger to invoke the Lambda function:

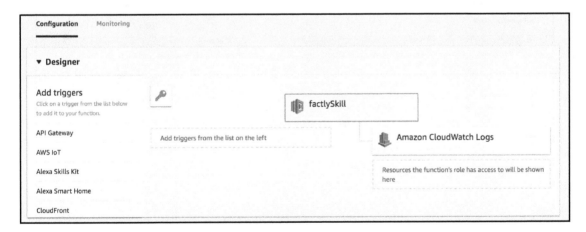

Figure 4.23: Configuring the Lambda

From the list of triggers on the left, select **Alexa Skills Kit** since Alexa will be invoking and supplying input to our Lambda function:

Figure 4.24: Adding a trigger for the Lambda

Once we have added the trigger, the next step will be to add the Skill ID that we copied in the previous section. Add the Skill ID in the section shown in the following screenshot:

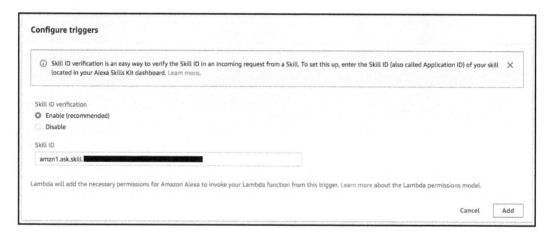

Figure 4.25: Adding the Skill ID to the Lambda

Adding the **Skill ID** ensures that the Lambda responds to only those requests that are generated by the verified skill. After adding the **Skill ID**, click on the **Add** button at the bottom of the screen and then on the **Save** button on the top-right corner of the screen.

3. Once you have clicked the **Save** button, select the `factlySkill` box under the **Designer** section, as shown in the following screenshot:

Figure 4.26: Concluding the Lambda configuration

This should bring up a code editor at the bottom where we will add the code for the Lambda.

Coding the Lambda function

We will be editing the code inline, in the `index.js` file in the developer portal itself:

1. First of all, we shall define an array of JSON, which will contain the quiz questions to be posed by the trivia skill. This can be defined right at the top of the `index.js` file, even before the `exports.handler`:

```
//questions is an array of json objects
var questions = [
    {
        "World War I began in which year?": [
            "1923",
            "1938",
            "1917",
            "1914"
        ]
    },
    {
        "Adolf Hitler was born in which country?": [
```

```
                              "France",
                              "Austria",
                              "Hungary",
                              "Germany"
                      ]
              },
              {
                  "The battle of Hastings was fought in which country?":
              [
                              "France",
                              "Russia",
                              "England",
                              "Norway"
                      ]
              }
      ];

      var correctAnswerSlots = [3, 1, 2];
```

As shown in the preceding code, apart from the `questions` array, we have also defined another array called `correctAnswerSlots`, which contains the index of the correct answers for each question defined in the `questions` array.

Confused? We can elaborate this with an example. It can be deduced from the `correctAnswerSlots` array that the answer to the first question, `World War I began in which year?`, is `1914`, which is located at index `3` (or is the fourth choice). Hence, we have `3` in the first position in the `correctAnswerSlots` array.

2. Now, we can go ahead and implement the handling of events in `exports.handler`. Our Lambda will be handling two basic requests:

   - `LaunchRequest`: To handle the launch of the skill
   - `IntentRequest`: To handle various Intents (in our case, we have just two intents, the first one being the `Answer` intent, which indicates the answer of the quiz question posed by `Factly`, and `AMAZON.StopIntent`, which indicates an exit from the skill)

We shall start by segregating each of the requests that our skill receives. For this, declare the following handler:

```
exports.handler = function (event, context) {
    try {

        if (event.request.type === "LaunchRequest") {
        } else if (event.request.type === "IntentRequest") {
```

```
            }
        } catch (e) {
            context.fail("Exception: " + e);
        }
    };
```

This is how we segregate the `Launch` and `Intent` event requests.

3. Next up, we will define some helper functions that will help us in creating speech responses:

```
// ------- Helper functions -------

function buildSpeechletResponse(output, repromptText,
shouldEndSession) {
    return {
        outputSpeech: {
            type: "PlainText",
            text: output
        },
        reprompt: {
            outputSpeech: {
                type: "PlainText",
                text: repromptText
            }
        },
        shouldEndSession: shouldEndSession
    };
}

function buildResponse(sessionAttributes, speechletResponse) {
    return {
        version: "1.0",
        sessionAttributes: sessionAttributes,
        response: speechletResponse
    };
}
```

These functions help the Lambda in returning the response to be spoken by Alexa whenever it receives a specific intent/input.

The `buildResponse` function will generate the plain-spoken response to be spoken by Alexa.

The `buildSpeechletResponse` function will specify the output that Alexa will eventually speak, in the form of plain text. It also takes another variable, `shouldEndSession`, which specifies whether Alexa should end the session after the response or not.

4. Once we have the helper functions configured, we can update the handling of `LaunchRequest` and `IntentRequest` cases to have Alexa speak relevant responses, as shown in the following code:

```
exports.handler = function (event, context) {
    try {

        if (event.request.type === "LaunchRequest") {
            onLaunch(event.request,
                event.session,
                function callback(sessionAttributes,
speechletResponse) {
context.succeed(buildResponse(sessionAttributes,
speechletResponse));
                });
        } else if (event.request.type === "IntentRequest") {
            //TBD
        }
    } catch (e) {
        context.fail("Exception: " + e);
    }
};
```

When the Lambda receives a `LaunchRequest`, it will call the `onLaunch` method to send a welcome message back:

```
function onLaunch(launchRequest, session, callback) {
    getWelcomeResponse(callback);
}
```

We shall be implementing the `getWelcomeResponse` method in the next step.

Please save our progress by clicking the **Save** button in the top-right corner of the screen.

5. The `getWelcomeResponse` method is responsible for formulating the launch response and posing the first question to the user:

```
var ANSWER_COUNT = 4;
var GAME_LENGTH = 3;

function getWelcomeResponse(callback) {
    var sessionAttributes = {},
        speechOutput = "Factly will ask you " +
GAME_LENGTH.toString()
            + " questions, try to get as many right as you can.
Just say the number of the answer. Let's begin. ",
        shouldEndSession = false,


        gameQuestions = populateGameQuestions(),
        currentQuestionIndex = 0,
        correctAnswerIndex =
correctAnswerSlots[currentQuestionIndex],
        answers = populateAnswers(gameQuestions, 0),

        spokenQuestion =
Object.keys(questions[gameQuestions[currentQuestionIndex]])[0],
        repromptText = "Question 1. " + spokenQuestion + " ",

        i;

    for (i = 0; i < ANSWER_COUNT; i++) {
        repromptText += (i+1).toString() + ". " + answers[i] +
". "
    }
    speechOutput += repromptText;
    sessionAttributes = {
        "speechOutput": repromptText,
        "repromptText": repromptText,
        "currentQuestionIndex": currentQuestionIndex,
        "correctAnswerIndex": correctAnswerIndex + 1,
        "questions": gameQuestions,
        "score": 0
    };
    callback(sessionAttributes,
        buildSpeechletResponse(speechOutput, repromptText,
shouldEndSession));
}
```

As shown in the preceding code, before defining the getWelcomeResponse function, we declare two variables, ANSWER_COUNT and GAME_LENGTH, which indicate the number of answers per question and the total number of quiz questions in the game. These variables will be used by the getWelcomeResponse function.

Next, we define the getWelcomeResponse function, which first creates a launch response using the GAME_LENGTH variable. It then loads all the indices for gameQuestions using the populateGameQuestions method:

```
function populateGameQuestions() {
    var gameQuestions = [];
    var index = questions.length;

    if (GAME_LENGTH > index){
        throw "Invalid Game Length.";
    }

    for (var j = 0; j < GAME_LENGTH; j++){
        gameQuestions.push(j);
    }

    return gameQuestions;
}
```

It later uses this to populate the answers for each question using the populateAnswers method:

```
function populateAnswers(gameQuestionIndexes,
correctAnswerIndex) {
    var answers =
questions[gameQuestionIndexes[correctAnswerIndex]][Object.keys(
questions[gameQuestionIndexes[correctAnswerIndex]])[0]];

    var index = answers.length;

    if (index < ANSWER_COUNT){
        throw "Not enough answers for question.";
    }

    return answers;
}
```

It also sets the `currentQuestionIndex` to 0 (since this is the very first question to be posed by the Factly Skill) before creating the `sessionAttributes` and finally creating the `speechletResponse` to be passed back to Alexa.

6. With the handling of the `onLaunch` method in place, we will now focus on the `onIntent` method, which gets called once the Lambda receives an `IntentRequest`:

```
exports.handler = function (event, context) {
    try {
        if (event.request.type === "LaunchRequest") {
            onLaunch(event.request,
                event.session,
                function callback(sessionAttributes,
speechletResponse) {
context.succeed(buildResponse(sessionAttributes,
speechletResponse));
                });
        } else if (event.request.type === "IntentRequest") {
            onIntent(event.request,
                event.session,
                function callback(sessionAttributes,
speechletResponse) {
context.succeed(buildResponse(sessionAttributes,
speechletResponse));
                });
        }
    } catch (e) {
        context.fail("Exception: " + e);
    }
};
```

The `onIntent` method handles the only two intents raised by the Factly Skill:

```
function onIntent(intentRequest, session, callback) {

    var intent = intentRequest.intent,
        intentName = intentRequest.intent.name;

    if ("Answer" === intentName) {
        handleAnswerRequest(intent, session, callback);
    } else if ("AMAZON.StopIntent" === intentName) {
        handleFinishSessionRequest(intent, session, callback);
    } else {
        throw "Invalid intent";
    }
}
```

We shall first see the simpler of the two, which is AMAZON.StopIntent, raised once the user decides to prematurely end the skill's execution by saying a phrase such as "Alexa, Stop Factly." This causes handleFinishSessionRequest to be called:

```
function handleFinishSessionRequest(intent, session, callback)
{
    callback(session.attributes,
        buildSpeechletResponse("Factly will Exit. Good bye!",
"", true));
}
```

This says a goodbye phrase to the user before the Factly Skill exits.

The Answer intent request is a significantly more complicated one, as it has multiple information flow paths and is handled by the handleAnswerRequest method:

```
function handleAnswerRequest(intent, session, callback) {
    var speechOutput = "";
    var sessionAttributes = {};
    var gameInProgress = session.attributes &&
session.attributes.questions;
    var answerSlotValid = isAnswerSlotValid(intent);
    var userGaveUp = intent.name === "DontKnowIntent";


    {
        var gameQuestions = session.attributes.questions,
            correctAnswerIndex =
parseInt(session.attributes.correctAnswerIndex),
            currentScore = parseInt(session.attributes.score),
            currentQuestionIndex =
parseInt(session.attributes.currentQuestionIndex),
            correctAnswerText =
session.attributes.correctAnswerText;

        var speechOutputAnalysis = "";

        if (answerSlotValid &&
parseInt(intent.slots.Choice.value) == correctAnswerIndex) {
            currentScore++;
            speechOutputAnalysis = "correct. ";
        } else {
            if (!userGaveUp) {
                speechOutputAnalysis = "wrong. ";
            }
            speechOutputAnalysis += "The correct answer is . .
```

```
. " + correctAnswerIndex;
        }
        // if we reached end of quiz and can exit the game
session
        if (currentQuestionIndex == GAME_LENGTH - 1) {
            speechOutput = userGaveUp ? "" : "That answer is .
. ";
            speechOutput += speechOutputAnalysis + " . . You
got . . . " + currentScore.toString() + " out of "
                + GAME_LENGTH.toString() + " questions correct.
Thank you for playing!";
            callback(session.attributes,
                buildSpeechletResponse(speechOutput, "",
true));
        } else {
            currentQuestionIndex += 1;
            var spokenQuestion =
Object.keys(questions[gameQuestions[currentQuestionIndex]])[0];
            correctAnswerIndex =
correctAnswerSlots[currentQuestionIndex];
            var answers = populateAnswers(gameQuestions,
currentQuestionIndex),

                questionIndexForSpeech = currentQuestionIndex +
1,
                repromptText = "Question " +
questionIndexForSpeech.toString() + ". " + spokenQuestion + "
";
            for (var i = 0; i < ANSWER_COUNT; i++) {
                repromptText += (i+1).toString() + " . " +
answers[i] + " . "
            }
            speechOutput += userGaveUp ? "" : "That answer is .
. ";
            speechOutput += speechOutputAnalysis + " . . . .
Your score is " + currentScore.toString() + ". . ." +
repromptText;

            sessionAttributes = {
                "speechOutput": repromptText,
                "repromptText": repromptText,
                "currentQuestionIndex": currentQuestionIndex,
                "correctAnswerIndex": correctAnswerIndex + 1,
                "questions": gameQuestions,
                "score": currentScore
            };
            callback(sessionAttributes,
                buildSpeechletResponse(speechOutput,
```

```
repromptText, false));
        }
    }
}
```

The preceding method first checks whether the answer/choice provided by the user is actually a valid one using the `isAnswerSlotValid` method:

```
function isAnswerSlotValid(intent) {
    var answerSlotFilled = intent.slots && intent.slots.Choice
&& intent.slots.Choice.value;
    var answerSlotIsInt = answerSlotFilled &&
!isNaN(parseInt(intent.slots.Choice.value));
    return answerSlotIsInt &&
parseInt(intent.slots.Choice.value) < (ANSWER_COUNT + 1) &&
parseInt(intent.slots.Choice.value) > 0;
}
```

This basically checks whether the answer provided by the user is a valid integer and is within the valid answer range.

Then, it goes on to verify the answer is actually correct using the `correctAnswerIndex` variable associated with the session attributes that we created in *Step 5*. It then checks whether the game has actually ended or the user is continuing to another question before creating the final `speechletResponse`.

After we have added the final piece of code in the `index.js` file, save progress by clicking the **Save** button in the top-right corner of the screen.

7. Now, we need to link the Lambda to our skill and, for this purpose, we will need the ARN of our Lambda. The ARN is located in the top-right corner of the Lambda function/code editor page. Copy the ARN and once you have copied the ARN, navigate to the previous browser tab, where we were configuring the Interaction Model of our skill via the **Skill builder checklist**. Select the **Endpoint** section to navigate to the **Endpoint** screen:

Figure 4.27: Adding the Lambda ARN to the Factly Skill

As shown in the preceding screenshot, select **AWS Lambda ARN** as **Service Endpoint Type** and enter the ARN that we copied earlier (shown obfuscated in the preceding screenshot due to privacy and security reasons).

Select the **Save Endpoints** button, navigate to **Skill builder checklist** and rebuild the model again.

Adding Persistence to Factly

When it comes to games (and also to life), persistence is the key. Seriously, if we had no way to save the progress of Mario at different levels, we would have never ended up saving the princess eventually.

To know more about Mario, please visit `https://en.wikipedia.org/wiki/Mario`.

We can also add persistence to any Alexa Skill for saving the current state or the user's progress. Saving state can be used as a delighter or it can also be a necessity, especially in **Game/Entertainment**-oriented skills where it is critical to save the user's progress.

In this section, we shall demonstrate adding persistence to Factly; we shall be informing the user of the number of times they have played Factly up until now, and for this we will be storing the launch count using **DynamoDB**, which is a NoSQL database service provided by AWS.

 To read more about DynamoDB, please navigate to https://aws.amazon.com/dynamodb/.

We will be accessing DynamoDB via our Lambda code to persist and retrieve the launch counter. However, our Lambda, in its current state, cannot connect to DynamoDB. You may now ask: why so? The reason is that our Lambda, in its current state, is executing in **lambda_basic_execution** mode, which we chose while creating it, and this mode only allows the Lambda to execute some basic code and log some data. To connect to DynamoDB, we will need to elevate **lambda_basic_execution** mode so that it can access DynamoDB and we will do this via **IAM**, which is an Amazon Web Service for **Identity and Access Management**.

 To know more about IAM, please visit https://aws.amazon.com/iam/.

Let's get started:

1. Navigate to https://console.aws.amazon.com. From the list of provided services, select **IAM** and, if you cannot find it, then just search for it in the search box provided, as shown in the following screenshot:

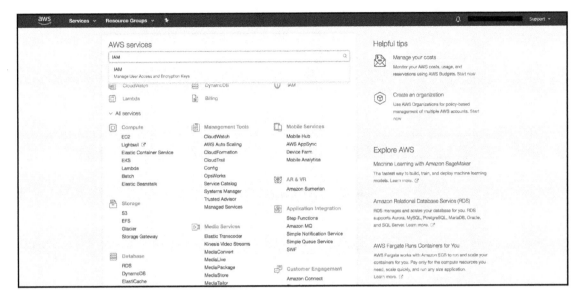

Figure 4.28: Navigation to IAM on AWS console

Please select **IAM** to navigate to the IAM dashboard.

2. Once on the IAM dashboard, please select **Roles** from the left menu:

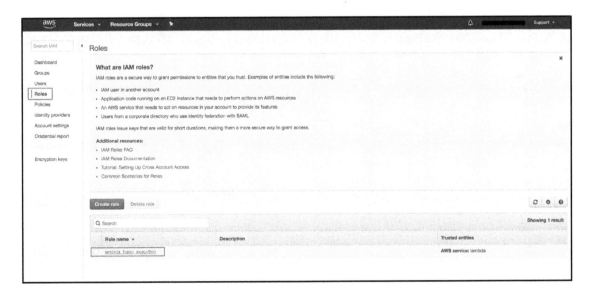

Figure 4.29: IAM roles

On the **Roles** screen, you should have a pre-existing **lambda_basic_execution** role, since we have been using it for all our Lambda functions. Click on it; we are going to augment it with a policy so that we can access DynamoDB with this role. This way, we will not need to make any additional configuration changes (for example, creating a new role from scratch).

3. On the next screen, click the **Attach policy** button:

Figure 4.30: Attaching a policy

You will land on the policy list. Search using `DynamoDB` to find the list of available policies for accessing DynamoDB:

Figure 4.31: Choosing the correct policy for DynamoDB access

Select the **AmazonDynamoDBFullAccess** policy. Finally, click on the **Attach policy** button at the bottom of the screen.

Now, our Lambda function should be able to access DynamoDB. Next up, we shall create a table in DynamoDB to store the launch counter values.

4. Now, navigate to `https://console.aws.amazon.com` again and, from the list of provided services, select **DynamoDB**. If you cannot find it, then just search for it in the search box provided:

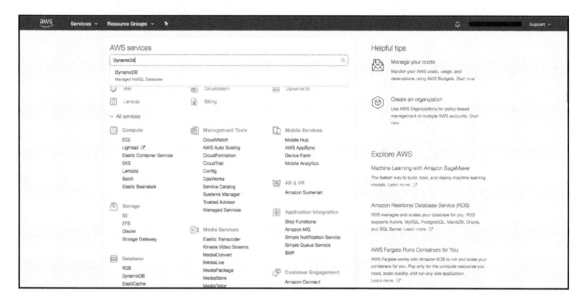

Figure 4.32: Navigating to DynamoDB

Select **DynamoDB** to navigate to the DynamoDB dashboard.

5. On the DynamoDB dashboard, click the **Create table** button to land on the **Create DynamoDB table** screen:

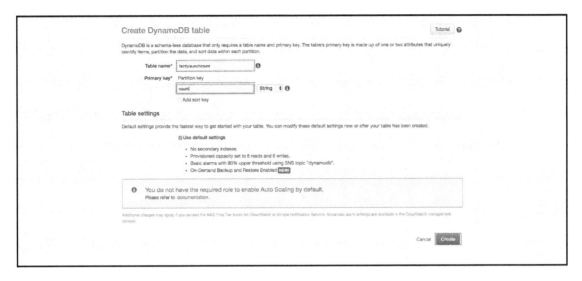

Figure 4.33: Creating the DynamoDB table

As shown in the preceding screenshot, provide the table name `factlylaunchcount` and the primary key `count`. Click on the **Create** button when done.

6. Clicking on **Create** should create the table after a momentarily delay and should bring up the details screen for the `factlylaunchcount` table:

Figure 4.34: DynamoDB table configuration

The table by default is configured to **5** read/writes per second, which is OK for our developmental purposes but should be updated as we scale up our skill.

We now need to add the actual launch counter variable, which will store our launch count. Click on the **Items** tab highlighted in the preceding screenshot.

7. Under the **Items** tab, click on the **Create item** button to bring up the **Create item** window:

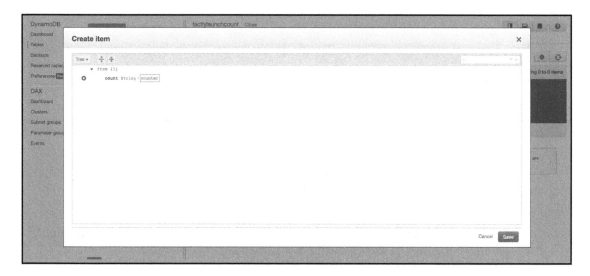

Figure 4.35: Adding items/keys to DynamoDB table

In the **Create item** window, provide the count primary key with a value of `counter`, as shown in the preceding screenshot.

8. Next, in the same window, select the + button to **Insert** a new column in the table with the type **Number**, as shown in the following screenshot:

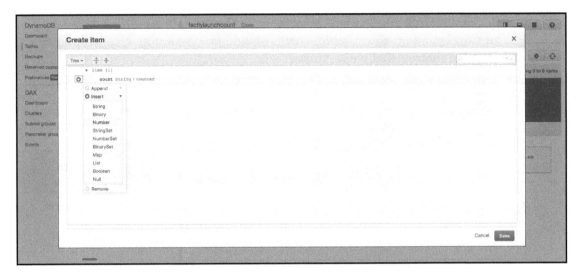

Figure 4.36: Adding new columns to DynamoDB table

Please name this new column `launchcounter` and give it an initial value of `0`:

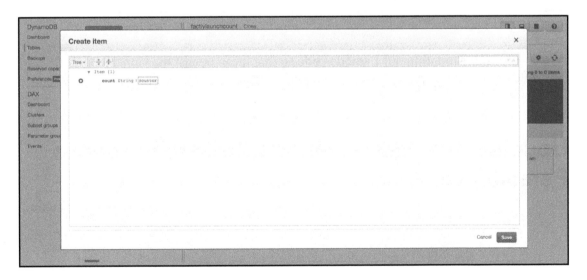

Figure 4.37: Naming the new columns in the DynamoDB table

Click on the **Save** button at the bottom of the **Create item** window when done. The `factlylaunchcount` table schema should now be automatically updated to reflect the changes that we just made:

Figure 4.38: Changes being reflected in DynamoDB table

We can now start updating our Lambda code so that it can persist the launch counter. Navigate back to our Lambda code, so that we can update it to include the persistence of launch counter.

Updating the Factly Lambda Code to Introduce Persistence

We shall start the modification of the Lambda code by including the AWS dependency first:

1. Add the following lines of code in the very beginning of the Lambda code (the `index.js` file):

```
var AWS = require('aws-sdk');
var docClient = new AWS.DynamoDB.DocumentClient();
```

Here, we include the AWS SDK and then use it to get an instance of the `DynamoDB.DocumentClient` instance, which will help us in reading and writing data to and from DynamoDB.

2. Next, modify the `onLaunch` method from the one given in the following code (which we wrote earlier):

```
function onLaunch(launchRequest, session, callback) {
    getWelcomeResponse(callback);
}
```

Modify it to this:

```
function onLaunch(launchRequest, session, callback) {
    var paramsGet = {
        TableName: 'factlylaunchcount',
        Key: {
            count: "counter"
        }
    };

    docClient.get(paramsGet, function(err, data) {
        if (err) {
            console.log("Error occurred:" + err);
        } else {
            var initialLaunchCount = data.Item.launchcounter;
            var updatedCount = initialLaunchCount + 1;
            var paramsUpdate = {
                TableName: 'factlylaunchcount',
                Key: {
                    count: "counter"
                },
                AttributeUpdates: {
                    launchcounter: {
                        Action: "PUT",
                        Value: updatedCount
                    }
                }
            }
        }
        docClient.update(paramsUpdate, function(err, data) {
            if (err) {
                console.log("Error occurred:" + err)
            } else {
                console.log("Data Put Success:" + data);
            }
            getWelcomeResponse(callback, initialLaunchCount);
        });
    });
}
```

Let's break down the preceding piece of code to understand what we are doing. So, earlier, when we launched the app, we provided a hardcoded response to the user via the `getWelcomeResponse` method. However, with the introduction of persistence, things are a little different now. We first define some parameters, that is, `paramsGet`, to fetch the data from the table. These parameters include the following:

- The `TableName` from where the data should be fetched
- The specific item to be fetched based on a `Key`; we are essentially saying "Please fetch the item from the `factlylaunchcount` table where primary key is `counter`"

Once the item is fetched, we extract the value of `launchcounter` from that item, which happens in this line:

```
var initialLaunchCount = data.Item.launchcounter;
```

Next, we increment the launch count by 1 and update it in the `factlylaunchcount` table via the call in the following code:

```
docClient.update(paramsUpdate, function(err, data)
```

After the update call, we pass `initialLaunchCount` to the `getWelcomeResponse` function.

3. Next, what remains is to update the signature of the `getWelcomeResponse` function from this:

```
function getWelcomeResponse(callback)
```

Update it to the one shown in the following code:

```
function getWelcomeResponse(callback, count)
```

We can now update the static response in the `getWelcomeResponse` function from the one shown in the following code:

```
speechOutput = "Factly will ask you " + GAME_LENGTH.toString()
            + " questions, try to get as many right as you can.
Just say the number of the answer. Let's begin. "
```

We update it to a dynamic response that takes into account the count variable:

```
speechOutput = "You have played Factly "+count.toString()+"
times. Factly will ask you " + GAME_LENGTH.toString()
             + " questions, try to get as many right as you can.
Just say the number of the answer. Let's begin. "
```

Now, the Factly Skill will be able to remember how many times it has been played by the user and will be able to notify the user about this.

Please find the code for the Lambda that specifically includes persistence at the following URL: https://github.com/madhurbhargava/AlexaSkillsProjects/blob/master/Chapter4_Factly_Persistence_index.js.

With our Lambda code now complete, now is the time to test it.

Testing the skill

Our skill is now complete and we are ready to test it. The skill can be tested via the actual Amazon Echo device or via the Amazon Service Simulator. We shall first test our skill via the Amazon Service Simulator and then via an actual Amazon Echo device.

On the **Test** page, scroll down to the Service Simulator and enter the Alexa, Launch Factly text, as shown in the following screenshot:

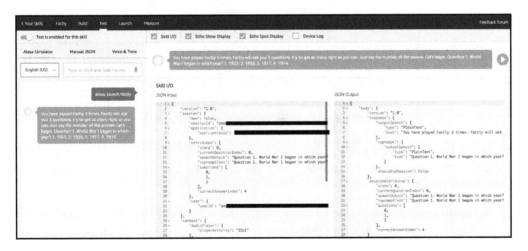

Figure 4.39: Testing the Factly Skill via the Amazon Service Simulator, step 1

If you look closely at Alexa's response, then you can already see that it has included the launch count, which it has fetched from DynamoDB along with the response launch phrase and the first question.

Then, you can simply enter an answer number (for example, 4 and the test simulator will let you know whether the answer is correct or not along with the next question, as shown in the following screenshot:

Figure 4.40: Testing the Factly Skill via the Amazon Service Simulator, step 2

Alternatively, you can also test the skill using Amazon Echo, provided the Echo is connected and set up:

- If you say: "Alexa, launch Factly," it should reply with: "You have played Factly *n* times. Factly will ask you three questions, try to get as many right as you can. Just say the number of the answer. Let's begin. Question 1. World War I began in which year? 1. 1923; 2. 1938; 3. 1917; 4. 1914."

- Then it will continue depending on your reply.
- You can end the gameplay at any point in time by simply saying: "Alexa, stop Factly."

Our skill is now tested and ready to be played around with. You can find the code of the Lambda for this chapter at the link mentioned in the following information box.

 Please find the code for the Lambda at the following URL: `https://github.com/madhurbhargava/AlexaSkillsProjects/blob/master/Chapter4_Factly_index.js`.

Summary

We do hope that you enjoyed creating the Factly Skill. As with the previous skills, the Factly Skill still has room for a lot of improvement. For example, currently it only hosts three questions, which can be extended to 30 or even 300 questions, and that alone will convert this skill to a serious quiz game.

Also, we are only handling two intents. We can extend the skill to handle even more intents, which can deal with the repetition of questions and other sorts of replies from users (for example, "I don't know," "Pass," or "Next question").

Persistence with DynamoDB was something brand new that we introduced and learned about in this chapter, and the idea itself can be extended to persist multiple things such as user scores, user progress, and overall game state. We left these improvements as an exercise for the user to hone their skills even further.

In the next chapter, we will extend our Alexa knowledge even further by creating an Alexa Skill that is more oriented towards something that is currently taking the whole world by storm.

Can you guess what it is? Turn to the next chapter to find out.

5
Making Alexa Talk About CryptoCurrencies

"The future is here. It's just not widely distributed yet."

– *William Gibson*

We designed a trivia game, called Factly, with Alexa in the last chapter. In this chapter, as promised, we are going to work on something that, at the time of writing this book, has taken the whole world by storm and, as you may have guessed from the chapter's title, it is cryptocurrencies.

In this chapter, we will be building a Skill called `CryptoOracle` (yes, we do understand it is a bad naming choice both in terms of syntax, semantics, and Alexa Skill-naming rules, but since we are not going to publish it yet, we are going to stick with this name) that can make Alexa talk about the latest prices of various cryptocurrencies. We will cover the following topics in this chapter:

- A Brief Introduction to Cryptocurrencies
- Designing the CryptoOracle skill
- Building the CryptoOracle skill

Let's begin.

A Brief Introduction to Cryptocurrencies

For those who came late and missed the massive hype that Bitcoin and other similar cryptocurrencies, generated especially during 2017 and onward: cryptocurrencies are digital/virtual currencies, that is, unlike physical currencies, such as the dollar, euro or rupee, cryptocurrencies exist just as entries in a distributed database (usually). Various cryptographic techniques are deployed to record cryptocurrency transactions and their generation, and so these digital currencies are generically known as cryptocurrencies.

 Since cryptographic techniques are beyond the scope of this book, we won't be covering them here.

As of the time of writing this chapter, there are more than 1,500 cryptocurrencies available, and the *better* cryptocurrencies out of those 1,500 cryptocurrencies serve a unique purpose.

 You can check the number of known/traded cryptocurrencies by navigating to CoinMarketCap at `https://coinmarketcap.com/`.

Some cryptocurrencies are used as a medium of exchanging value, such as Bitcoin, Litecoin, Monero, and Dash. Other cryptocurrencies, such as Ethereum, are used to power distributed systems, such as the Ethereum Virtual Machine:

Currency	Purpose
Bitcoin	Medium of value exchange
Monero	Medium of value exchange focused on privacy
Ethereum	Used to power the Ethereum Virtual Machine
Litecoin	Faster and improved version of Bitcoin

One of the major reasons why cryptocurrencies are drawing so much attention is due to the speculative nature of their prices. Cryptocurrency prices rise and fall just like stock prices, and this draws a lot of attention from the general public and investors who speculate on the prices.

 Please note that the information presented in this section, regarding speculation on cryptocurrency prices, is just to provide information to our readers and is not investment advice.

Due to the preceding reasons, cryptocurrencies have become all the rage, hence we decided to focus this chapter on designing a skill that can help an Alexa user to enquire about cryptocurrency prices on the fly.

Designing the CryptoOracle skill

Now that we know what cryptocurrencies are and why are they are getting all the attention lately, we can design the CryptoOracle skill.

CryptoOracle will work via the following steps:

1. A user launches the skill:

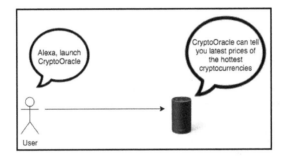

Figure 5.1: Launching the CryptoOracle skill

The launch response is fetched from the Lambda and played to the user, as shown in the preceding diagram.

2. A user asks Alexa about the price of any cryptocurrency:

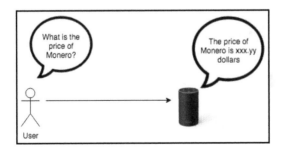

Figure 5.2: Querying the cryptocurrency price via the CryptoOracle skill

This request will do in the following:

- Launch an intent to fetch the price with the cryptocurrency name as a parameter
- The Lambda receives the intent and extracts the cryptocurrency name
- The Lambda fetches the cryptocurrency price via the coinmarketcap API using the currency name

To know more about the coinmarketcap API, navigate to `https://coinmarketcap.com/`.

Finally, the response from the Lambda, which contains the cryptocurrency price, is played to the user.

3. Optionally, the user can also ask CryptoOracle to stop/exit at any point of time during the dialog:

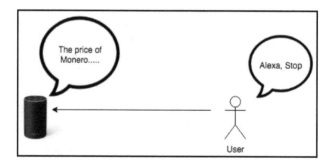

Figure 5.3: User-initiated exit from the CryptoOracle skill

In that case, the skill will stop its response midway and exit.

The complete interaction can be mapped out via a VUI-flow diagram:

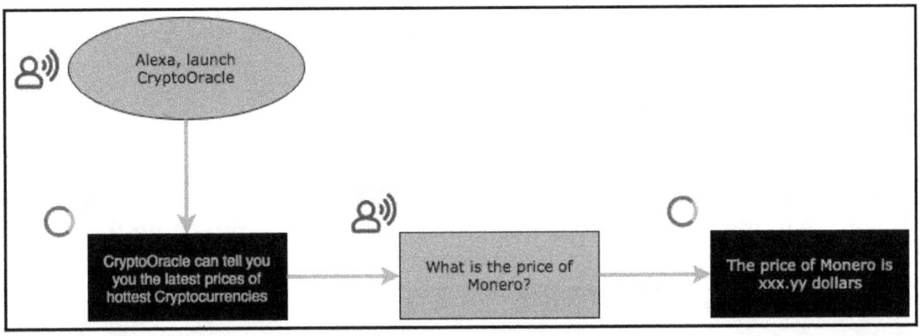

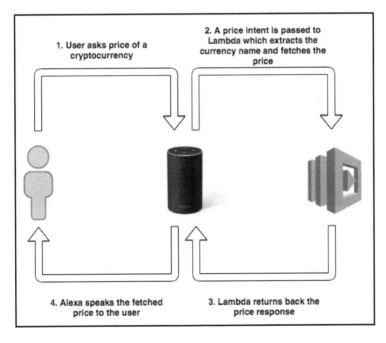

Figure 5.4: VUI-flow diagram for the CryptoOracle skill

The overall information flow of a typical session can be mapped out as shown in the following diagram:

Figure 5.5: Information flow in the CryptoOracle skill

With our data flow in place, it is now time to code the actual `CryptoOracle` skill.

Building the CryptoOracle skill

As of the time of writing this chapter, Amazon has recently updated its **Alexa Skills Kit (ASK)** developer console. We will be making use of the updated developer console for the purpose of developing our `CryptoOracle` skill:

1. Navigate to the ASK console at `https://developer.amazon.com/alexa`, **Sign In** to the portal, and go to the **Skills** creation page (we have already done this exercise in the previous chapters, hence we won't be repeating those steps):

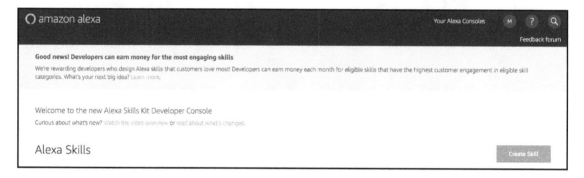

Figure 5.6: Alexa Skills Portal – ASK Console

Click on the **Create Skill** button located at the bottom of the screen.

2. The **Create a new skill** screen requires a **SkillName** to proceed further, as shown in the following screenshot:

Figure 5.7: Naming the CryptoOracle skill

Name our skill `CryptoOracle` and click on the **Next** button.

3. The next page will display the types of pre-built interaction models that can be added to the skill. Click on the **Select** button under the **Custom** model to select it, and click on the **Create Skill** button in the top-right corner of the screen.

4. After skill creation, we will need to configure its **Interaction Model** via the dashboard shown in the following screenshot:

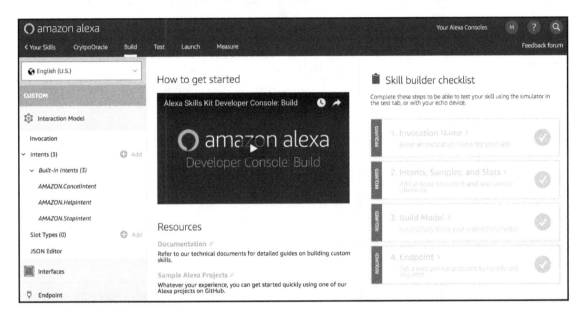

Figure 5.8: Interaction Model dashboard

We will configure the **Interaction Model** by completing the **Skill builder checklist**.

5. Select the first option, **Invocation Name**, under the **Skill builder checklist** to get to the screen shown in the following screenshot:

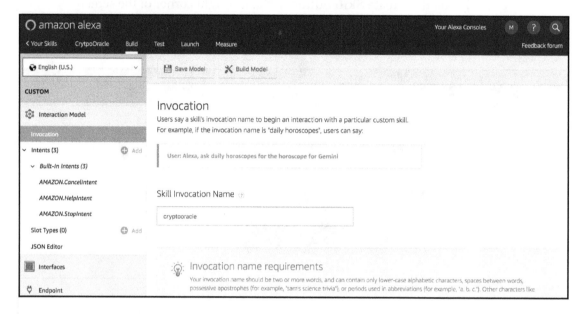

Figure 5.9: Adding the Invocation Name

Enter the **Skill Invocation Name** as `cryptooracle` and click on **Save Model** button in the top-left corner.

6. Click on the **Build** tab item to end up on the **Skill builder checklist**, which should have the **Invocation Name** option as marked and selected since we just completed setting it up:

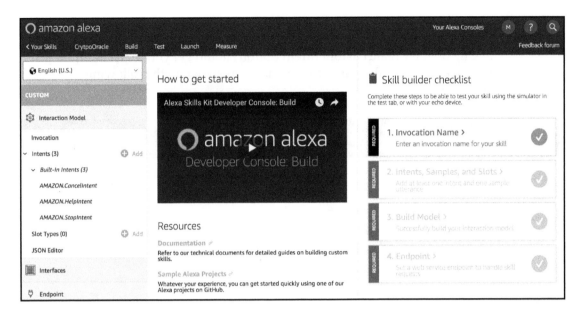

Figure 5.10: Successful Setup of the Invocation Name

Now, as our **Invocation Name** is set up, select the **Intents, Samples, and Slots** item from the checklist to get to the following screenshot:

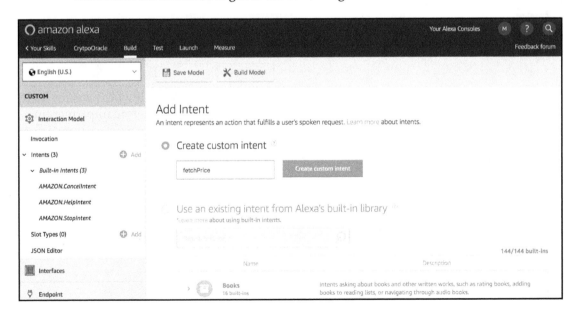

Figure 5.11: Setting up a custom intent

Name the intent `fetchPrice` and click on **Create custom intent** button.

7. Clicking on the **Create custom intent** button should get you to the **Sample Utterances** page for the `fetchPrice` intent, as shown in the following screenshot:

Figure 5.12: Naming the custom intent

Since all of our **Sample Utterances** will require a slot, through which we can pass the cryptocurrency name to the Lambda, we will add a slot before implementing the utterances.

Select the **Add** button next to the **Slot Types** under the **Intents** menu:

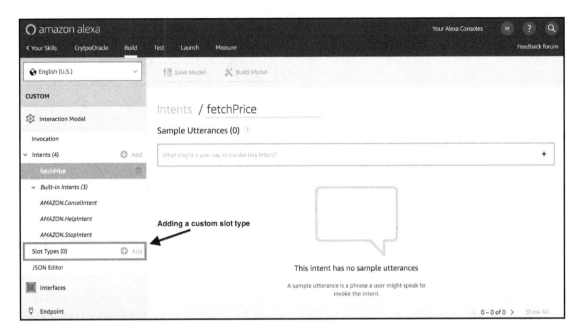

Figure 5.13: Adding a slot type to the custom intent

These should get you to the **Add Slot Type** page, as shown in the following screenshot:

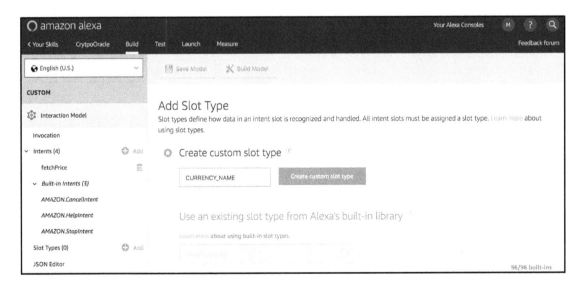

Figure 5.14: Naming the custom slot type for the intent

Under **Create custom slot type**, add a new slot type name as CURRENCY_NAME and click on the **Create custom slot type** button.

8. Clicking on the **Create custom slot type** button brings up the **Slot Values** screen:

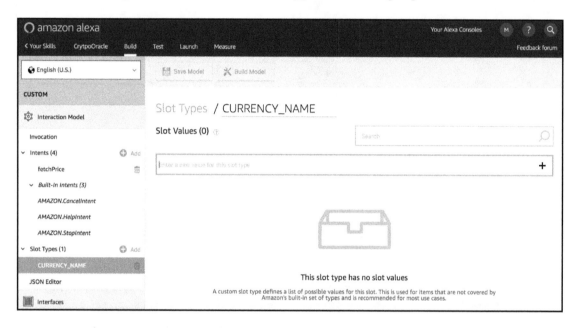

Figure 5.15: Adding slot values – step 1

Since our CURRENCY_NAME slot will hold the cryptocurrency name, the price of which the user needs to retrieve:

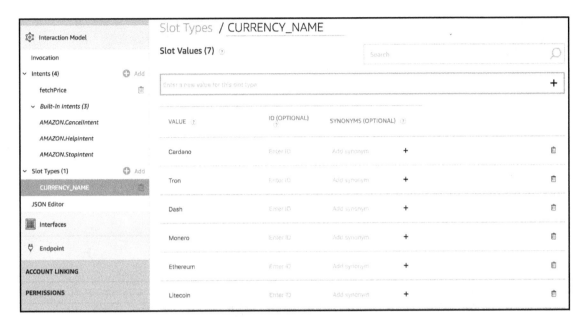

Figure 5.16: Adding slot values – step 2

As shown in the preceding screenshot, add all the cryptocurrency names that you know under the **Slot Values** option. Note: this addition of slot values is optional as our Lambda will be able to extract any slot value and fetch its price.

9. With our **Slot Types** set up, we can now use the slot type to create a custom slot. Click on **fetchPrice** under the **Intents** dropdown:

Figure 5.17: Configuring the custom intent with the slot – step 1

Now, scroll toward the bottom of the page:

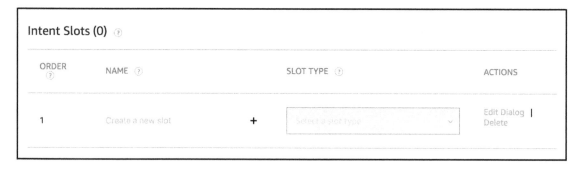

Figure 5.18: Configuring the custom intent with the slot – step 2

Under the **Intents Slots** option, create a new slot called `currencyName` and give it a custom type of CURRENCY_NAME, which we created earlier:

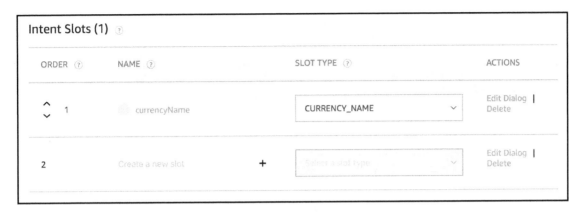

Figure 5.19: Configuring the custom intent with the slot – step 3

We can now use this slot in our `fetchPrice` intent schema.

10. With our **Intent Slots** set up, we are now ready to define the sample utterances for the `fetchPrice` intent. Scroll up the page and, before we do anything else, save the **Interaction Model** by clicking on the **Save Model** button:

Figure 5.20: Configuring the sample utterances – step 1

After saving the model, we can add a couple of utterances for our model, as shown in the following screenshot:

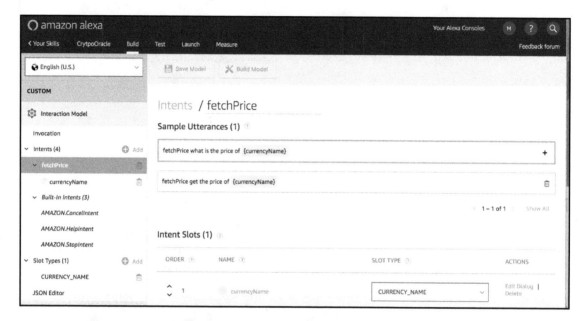

Figure 5.21: Configuring the sample utterances – step 2

All these utterances will use the `currencyName` slot that we defined earlier.

11. Once you have finished setting up the utterances, go ahead and select the **Build** tab to get to the dashboard:

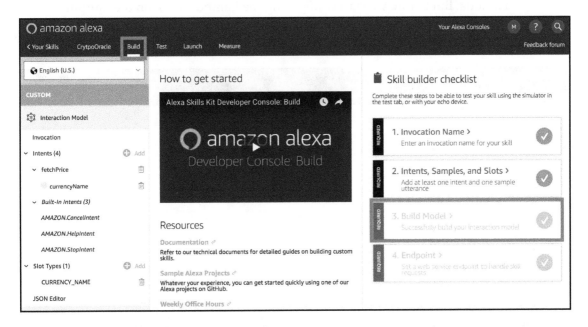

Figure 5.22: Building the interaction model

Finally, select the **Build Model** option to build the **Interaction Model**. The process should take a few minutes. The **Build Model** button on the dashboard should turn green after the build finishes successfully.

12. After the **Interaction Model** has finished building, we need to supply it with a Lambda Endpoint to connect to. We will postpone this step while we code our Lambda. But before we start configuring the Lambda, click on the **Endpoint** button on the dashboard shown in the preceding screenshot to navigate to the **Endpoint** screen:

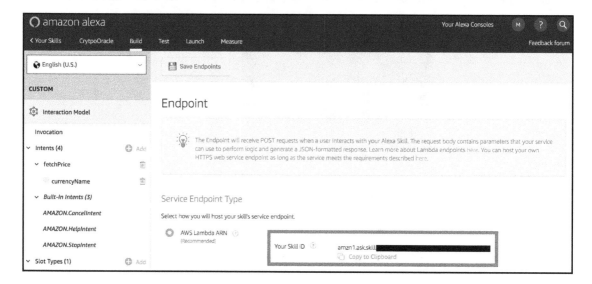

Figure 5.23: Copying the skill ID

Select **AWS Lambda ARN** from the given options, copy the skill ID from this page, and save it somewhere. We will need it shortly.

Configuring the Lambda function

Once the **Interaction Model** is created, we will leave the configuration dashboard as it is and focus on creating the Lambda:

1. Open a new browser tab and navigate to the AWS console.

 The AWS console can be found at `https://console.aws.amazon.com`. You may need to create a new account if you don't already have one.

Select **Lambda** under the **Compute** options. Click **Create function** on the next screen, name the function `cryptoOracleSkill`, and fill in the details:

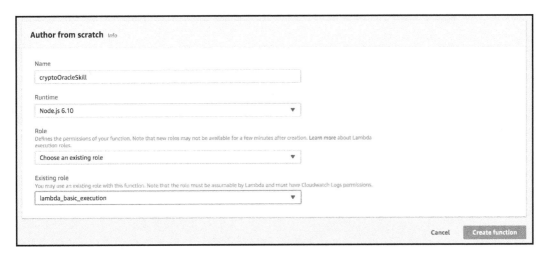

Figure 5.24: Naming the Lambda

Click on the **Create function** button after filling in the details.

2. Under the **Designer** section, you will need to add a trigger to invoke the Lambda function:

Figure 5.25: Configuring the Lambda

From the list of triggers on the left, select **Alexa Skills Kit** since Alexa will be invoking and supplying input to our Lambda function:

Figure 5.26: Adding a trigger for the Lambda

Once we have added the trigger, the next step is to add the skill ID that we copied in the previous section. Scroll to the bottom of the screen and add the **Skill ID** in the section shown in the following screenshot:

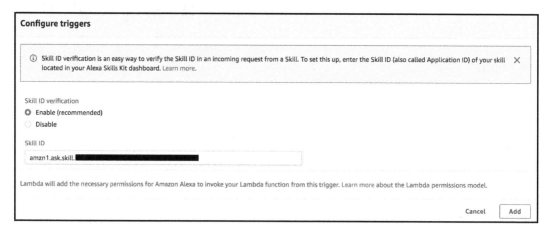

Fig 5.27: Adding the Skill ID to the Lambda

Adding the skill ID ensures that the Lambda responds to only those requests that are generated by the verified skill. After adding the **Skill ID**, click on the **Add** button at the bottom of the screen. Our Lambda configuration should have some unsaved changes now:

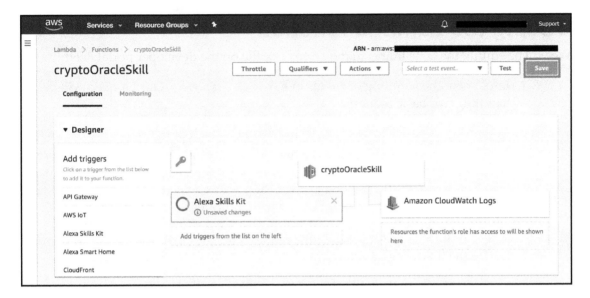

Figure 5.28: Saving changes to the Lambda

Save the recent changes by clicking on **Save** button in the top-right corner of the screen.

3. Once you have clicked the **Save** button, select the `cryptoOracleSkill` box under the **Designer** section:

Figure 5.29: Concluding the Lambda configuration

This should bring up a code editor where we will add the code for the Lambda.

Coding the Lambda function

We will be editing the code inline, in the `index.js` file on the developer portal itself:

1. Implement the handling of events in `exports.handler`. Our Lambda will be handling two basic requests:

   - `LaunchRequest`: To handle the launch of the skill
   - `IntentRequest`: To handle various intents (in our case we have just two intents, the first one being the `fetchPrice` intent, which asks the Lambda to fetch the price of a specific cryptocurrency, and `AMAZON.StopIntent`, which indicates an exit from the skill)

   We'll start by segregating each of the requests that our skill receives. For this, declare the following handler:

   ```javascript
   exports.handler = function (event, context) {
       try {

           if (event.request.type === "LaunchRequest") {
           } else if (event.request.type === "IntentRequest") {
           }
       } catch (e) {
           context.fail("Exception: " + e);
       }
   };
   ```

   As shown in the preceding code, this is how we segregate the launch and intent event requests.

2. Define some helper functions that will help us create speech responses, as shown in the following code:

   ```javascript
   // ------- Helper functions -------

   function buildSpeechletResponse(output, repromptText,
   shouldEndSession) {
       return {
           outputSpeech: {
               type: "PlainText",
               text: output
           },
           reprompt: {
               outputSpeech: {
   ```

```
                    type: "PlainText",
                    text: repromptText
              }
          },
          shouldEndSession: shouldEndSession
      };
  }

  function buildResponse(sessionAttributes, speechletResponse) {
      return {
          version: "1.0",
          sessionAttributes: sessionAttributes,
          response: speechletResponse
      };
  }
```

These functions help the Lambda to return the response to be spoken by Alexa whenever it receives a specific intent/input.

The `buildResponse` function will generate the spoken response to be uttered by Alexa.

The `buildSpeechletResponse` function will specify the output that Alexa will eventually speak, in the form of plain text. It also takes another `shouldEndSession` variable, which specifies whether Alexa should end the session after the response.

3. Once we configure the helper functions, we can update the handling of the `LaunchRequest` and `IntentRequest` cases to have Alexa say relevant responses:

```
exports.handler = function (event, context) {
    try {

        if (event.request.type === "LaunchRequest") {
            onLaunch(event.request,
                event.session,
                function callback(sessionAttributes,
speechletResponse) {
context.succeed(buildResponse(sessionAttributes,
speechletResponse));
                });
        } else if (event.request.type === "IntentRequest") {
            //TBD
        }
    } catch (e) {
```

```
            context.fail("Exception: " + e);
        }
    };
```

As shown in the preceding code, when the Lambda receives a `LaunchRequest`, it will call the `onLaunch` method to send a welcome message back:

```
function onLaunch(launchRequest, session, callback) {
    getWelcomeResponse(callback);
}
```

We will be implementing the< `getWelcomeResponse` method in the next step. Save your progress by clicking the **Save** button in the top-right corner of the screen.

4. The `getWelcomeResponse` method is responsible for formulating the launch response:

```
function getWelcomeResponse(callback) {
    var sessionAttributes = {},
        speechOutput = " Crypto Oracle can tell you latest
prices of the hottest cryptocurrencies",
        shouldEndSession = false,
        repromptText = "";
    callback(sessionAttributes,
        buildSpeechletResponse(speechOutput, repromptText,
shouldEndSession));
}
```

As shown in the preceding code, the method formulates a simple plain-text response for the launch message.

5. With the handling of the `onLaunch` method in place, we will now focus on the `onIntent` method, which gets called once the Lambda receives an `IntentRequest`:

```
exports.handler = function (event, context) {
    try {
        if (event.request.type === "LaunchRequest") {
            onLaunch(event.request,
                event.session,
                function callback(sessionAttributes,
speechletResponse) {
context.succeed(buildResponse(sessionAttributes,
speechletResponse));
                });
```

```
        } else if (event.request.type === "IntentRequest") {
            onIntent (event.request,
                event.session,
                function callback(sessionAttributes,
speechletResponse) {
context.succeed(buildResponse(sessionAttributes,
speechletResponse));
                });
        }
    } catch (e) {
        context.fail("Exception: " + e);
    }
};
```

The `onIntent` method handles the only two intents raised by the `CryptoOracle` skill:

```
function onIntent(intentRequest, session, callback) {
    var intent = intentRequest.intent,
        intentName = intentRequest.intent.name;

    if ("fetchPrice" === intentName) {
        handleRequest(intent, session, callback);
    } else if ("AMAZON.StopIntent" === intentName) {
        handleFinishSessionRequest(intent, session, callback);
    } else {
        throw "Invalid intent";
    }
}
```

We will first see the simpler of the two, `AMAZON.StopIntent`, which is raised once the user decides to prematurely end the skill's execution by saying a phrase such as, "Alexa, stop CrypoOracle." This causes `handleFinishSessionRequest` to be called:

```
function handleFinishSessionRequest(intent, session, callback)
{
    callback(session.attributes,
        buildSpeechletResponse("CryptoOracle will Exit. Good
bye!", "", true));
}
```

This utters a goodbye phrase to the user before the skill exits.

6. The `fetchPrice` intent request is slightly more complicated as it has multiple information-flow paths and is handled by the `handleRequest` method:

```
function handleRequest(intent, session, callback) {
    console.log("INSIDE Handle Request");
    var options = {
        host: 'api.coinmarketcap.com',
        port: 443,
        path: '/v1/ticker/' + intent.slots.currencyName.value +
"/" ,
        method: 'GET',
        headers: {
        'Content-Type': 'application/json'
        }
    };

    var req = https.request(options, function (res) {
        res.setEncoding('utf-8');
        var responseString = '';
        res.on('data', function (data) {
            responseString += data;
        });

        res.on('end', function () {
            var resp = JSON.parse(responseString);
            console.log(resp);
            var sessionAttributes = {},
        speechOutput = "The price of " +
intent.slots.currencyName.value + " is . . " +
resp[0].price_usd + " dollars",
            shouldEndSession = false,
            repromptText = "";
        callback(sessionAttributes,
            buildSpeechletResponse(speechOutput, repromptText,
shouldEndSession));
        });

    });

    req.end();
}
```

The `handleRequest` method extracts the slot from the intent and makes the request to the CoinMarketCap API, which then returns the information for the requested cryptocurrency.

If you need more information on the CoinMarketCap API, navigate to
`https://coinmarketcap.com/`.

Finally, the Lambda parses and formulates the received information from the CoinMarketCap API into a speech response.

As you can see, the preceding method uses the `https` variable, which is facilitating the retrieval of information from the CoinMarketCap API; we will declare it in the beginning of the `index.js` file, even before defining `exports.handler`:

```
var https = require('https');
```

After we have added the final piece of code in the `index.js` file, save your progress by clicking the **Save** button in the top-right corner of the screen.

7. We need to link the Lambda to our skill. For this purpose, we will need the ARN of our Lambda. The **ARN** is located in the top-right corner of the Lambda function/code editor page:

Figure 5.30: Copying the ARN

Copy the ARN and then navigate to the previous browser tab, where we were configuring the **Interaction Model** of our skill:

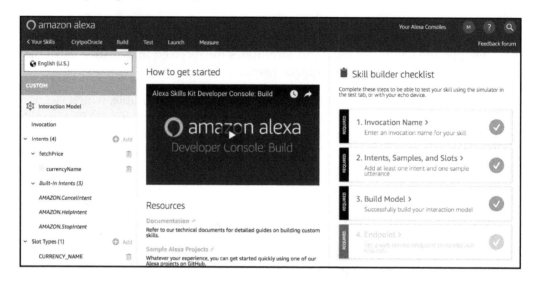

Figure 5.31: Updating the endpoint with ARN– step 1

Click on the **Endpoint** button under the **Skill builder checklist**, which should navigate you to the **Endpoint**, as shown in the following screenshot:

Figure 5.32: Updating the endpoint with ARN – step 2

Select **AWS Lambda ARN**; under the **Default Region** option, add the ARN that we copied from the previous screen, and click on the **Save Endpoints** button in the top-left corner of the screen.

After clicking on the **Save Endpoints** button, click on the **Build** tab to navigate to the dashboard.

8. On the dashboard, all the items in the **Skill builder checklist** should now be green:

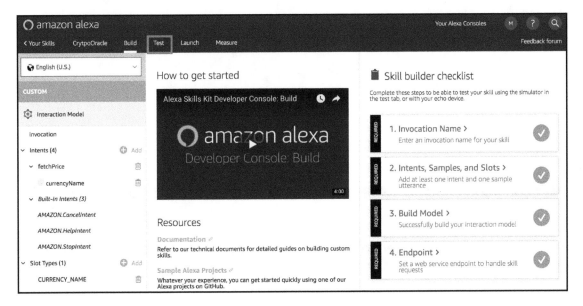

Fig 5.33: All steps green – skill ready

This indicates that our skill is now ready to be tested. Click on the **Test** tab, as shown in the preceding screenshot.

Testing the skill

The **Test** tab should bring up the Alexa simulator:

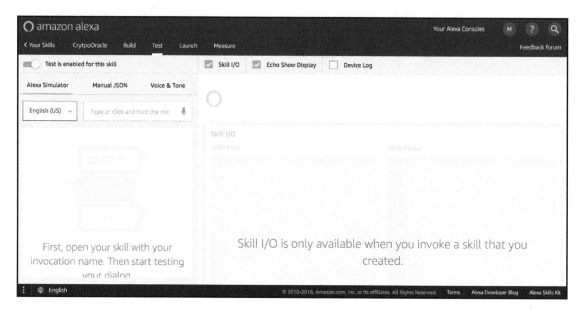

Fig 5.34: ASK simulator

The Alexa simulator greatly reduces the need for an actual Amazon Echo since you can easily test the `CryptoOracle` skill using just the simulator.

Enter `Alexa launch CryptoOracle` in the text box, as shown in the following screenshot, and press *Enter*:

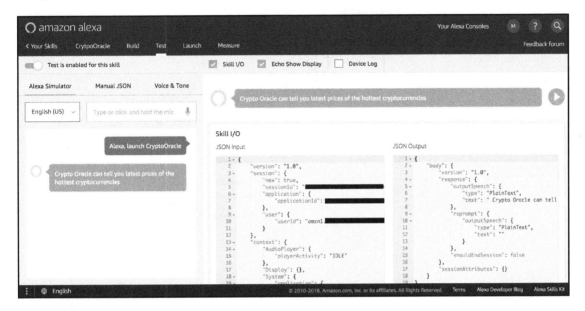

Figure 5.35: Launching the skill via the skill simulator

Alexa should reply with the correct response and, if the volume of your computer is turned on, you can even hear Alexa speaking that response.

You can now ask CryptoOracle for the price of your favorite cryptocurrency which it should successfully fetch and respond with:

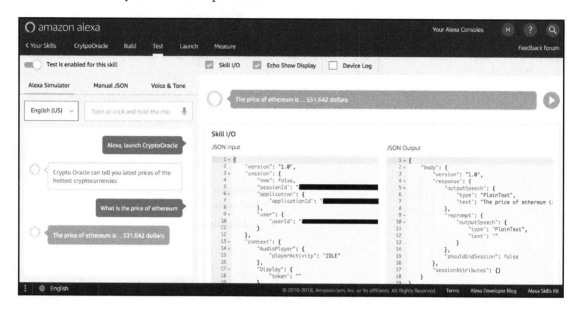

Figure 5.36: Querying the skill via the skill simulator

Our skill is now tested and ready to be played around with.

You can find the code for the Lambda at `https://github.com/madhurbhargava/AlexaSkillsProjects/blob/master/Chapter5_index.js`.

Summary

We hope you enjoyed creating the Crypto skill. As with the skills from the previous chapters, the `CryptoOracle` skill still has room for a lot of improvement. For example, currently it just fetches the price of a cryptocurrency, but you could easily modify it to fetch a lot of other parameters too. Hence we urge you to please take a closer look at the CoinMarketCap API to find out what all other parameters(for example, market cap, total supply, max supply, and so on) for a cryptocurrency it can be fetched so that you can augment the skill with more information.

Also, we are only handling two intents; we could extend the skill to handle even more intents that could deal with other user interactions.

We have left these improvements as an exercise for the user to hone their skill even further.

In the next chapter, we will extend our Alexa knowledge even further by creating an Alexa Skill that is oriented toward integrating Alexa with other smarthome devices.

Home Automation with Alexa

6

"Communication must be HOT. That's Honest, Open, and Two-Way."

– Dan Oswald

As we progress through this book, the skills we create are evolving too. We started with a simple Hello World Skill and went on to create an SMS sender, a trivia game, a skill that talks about cryptocurrencies, and in this chapter, we will be working on **Ambience Manager**, which can tell us the ambience parameters, such as the temperature and humidity, of our homes.

We will be designing this skill by covering the following topics:

- Introduction to Home Automation and Ambient Sensors
- Designing the Ambience Manager Skill
- Developing the Mobile App
- Developing the Ambience Manager Skill

This chapter will be covering a lot of ground since our **Ambience Manager** Skill will be communicating with an ambient sensor, hence it will also involve the details regarding the ambient sensor as well as a mobile app, which will help us in uploading the temperature data to the cloud.

Introduction to Home Automation and Ambient Sensors

For introductory purposes, home automation is a concept whereby a user can control standard home fixtures such as lights, music systems, televisions, and even climate, using an array of intelligent sensors rather than the traditional flipping of switches for each individual fixture. Home automation intends to keep the physical interaction of the user with the actual hardware as minimal as possible. In the recent present and the not-so-distant past, the concept of home automation was built on top of mobile operating systems (mostly Android or iOS), where the user was able to control the whole house using just a mobile device or a tablet rather than interacting with the switches of each individual device present in the house.

With the advent of Interactive Voice Assistants, the concept of home automation has transcended to the level where a user can control a home with just their voice. The actual concept of home automation is very broad and a complete solution will include a wide array of sensors. In this chapter, we will demonstrate the concept of home automation with respect to Voice-Based Personal Assistants using a key feature provided in almost every automated home, which is the gathering of information regarding climate/ambience (temperature, humidity, and so on). We will create a solution that includes an ambient sensor, a mobile app, and Alexa, from which a user can get the ambience details of their house by just asking Alexa.

Ambience monitoring solutions are not only used for home automation, but also in various warehouses (where it is imperative that the products are maintained at a certain temperature/humidity) due to the fact that they can transmit ambience data over long ranges, both over Wi-Fi and/or Bluetooth (BLE). However, those solutions are also more expensive and difficult to procure. Hence, for our needs, we will be using a popular sensor-prototyping solution called **CC2650STK** (popularly known as **SensorTag**) manufactured by Texas Instruments, that is small, easily available, perfectly fits with the home automation concept, and can be easily purchased from hobby/electronics stores or online from the **Texas Instruments Inc. (TI)** website, or Amazon, for a mere US$45-50.

 For more information, please refer to: `http://www.ti.com/tool/CC2650STK`

The CC2650STK, or the SensorTag, is even smaller than a credit card, operates on a single coin cell battery, and includes 10 low-power, tiny MEMS sensors:

- Light
- Digital microphone
- Magnetic sensor
- Humidity
- Magnetometer
- Pressure
- Accelerometer
- Gyroscope
- Ambient temperature
- Object temperature

All these sensors are assembled in a small package, the details of which are shown in the following diagram:

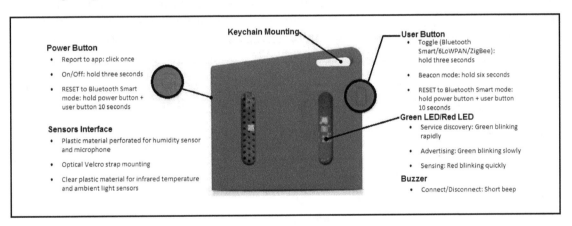

Figure 6.1: Elements of a CC2650STK

This sensor kit/SensorTag can sense a lot more than temperature, however, for the purpose of prototyping our skill, we'll just limit ourselves to interrogating the ambient temperature sensor.

The overall system that we will eventually develop will also include a mobile app, which will interact with the CC2650STK SensorTag over BLE and will upload the temperature readings to the Firebase backend.

 At the production level, we won't need the mobile app at all, as most practical sensors are fully capable and configured to upload data to backends over Wi-Fi. However, since we are prototyping, we are resorting to this solution.

Those readings can then be fetched from the Firebase backend by the Lambda and presented to the user when the user prompts Alexa for them.

Designing the Ambience Manager Skill

Our Ambience Manager Skill will have at least five moving parts, including a **User** that interacts with **Amazon Echo**, which in turns communicates with the **AWS Lambda**, which in turn fetches the temperature information from the **Firebase** cloud. The temperature information will be pushed to the Firebase cloud via the **Mobile Device**, which reads it from the **Ambient Sensor**. The flow of information is shown in the following diagram:

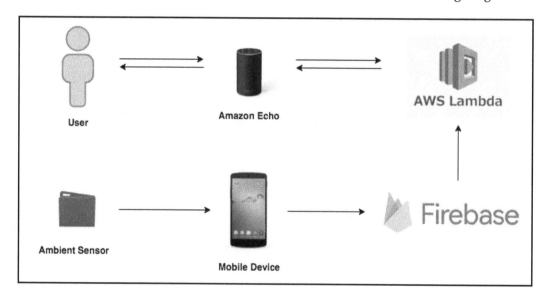

Figure 6.2: Data flow in Ambience Manager Skill

The ambient sensor will communicate the ambient parameters, that is, temperature and humidity, to a mobile app over BLE.

 To learn more about BLE, visit `https://www.bluetooth.com/news/` `pressreleases/2009/12/17/sig-introduces-bluetooth-low-energy-` `wireless-technologythe-next-generation-of-bluetooth-wireless-` `technology`.

This will eventually upload the ambient parameters to the Firebase backend.

 Firebase is a real-time database by Google. To learn more about Firebase, visit `https://firebase.google.com/`.

Once the data is available on the Firebase backend, the user will be communicating with the skill as follows:

Figure 6.3: One-Shot Launch for Ambience Manager Skill

Do you notice something different?

If you have not already noticed, we did not launch the skill (as we did for all the previous Alexa skills that we created), and yet went ahead to ask about the room temperature directly. This is what is known as **One-Shot Launch**, *which is when a user launches a skill and requests some information from it.* We will be covering the One-Shot Launch/Invocation in detail once we design/code the actual skill.

If the One-Shot Launch was successful, the Ambience Manager should reply with the correct temperature:

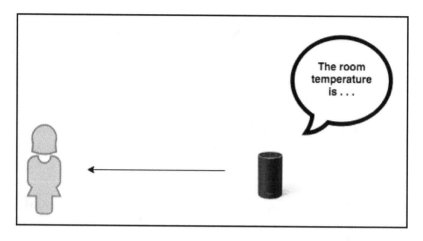

Figure 6.4: Dialog flow For Ambience Manager Skill

So much for the user interaction. The overall information flow of a typical session can be mapped out as shown in the following diagram:

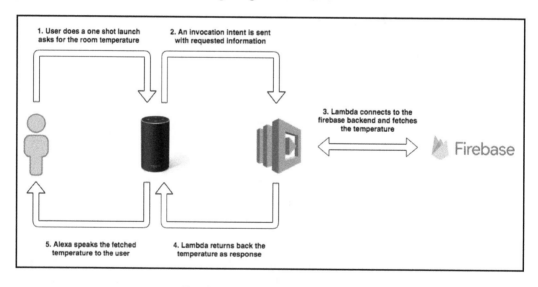

Figure 6.5: Skill operation for Ambience Manager Skill

With our data flow in place, we now take the next step: creating an Android app that will read data from the ambient sensor via BLE and then push that data to the Firebase backend.

Developing the Mobile App

We will be creating an Android app that will communicate with the ambient sensor over BLE.

If you do not know much about developing Android apps and BLE, don't worry, you can simply download the source code from the link provided toward the end of this section. Alternatively, you can check out the Android Developer website regarding the development of Android apps.

 If you are interested in exploring Android, navigate to `https://developer.android.com/` to find more information on Android app development.

The following are the prerequisites for this section:

- **Android**:
    - Latest Android Studio
    - An up-to-date Android device (preferably a Samsung Galaxy S8, since it has support for Bluetooth 5, otherwise any device with an API Level of 23 (Android M) is fine)
    - Basic familiarity with Java, Android, Android Studio, and BLE
- **Hardware**:
    - Texas Instruments CC2650 STK SensorTag

We'll begin by creating an empty project. Please choose a name for it.

For the purpose of consistency, and since this project has already been covered in another book of mine (titled *IoT Projects with Bluetooth Low Energy* published by Packt Publishing), I will call it `AndroidWarehouseMonitor`.

Since we are about to implement a lot of code for our Android app, for your convenience, we have broken down the functionality of the Android app in the following flowchart:

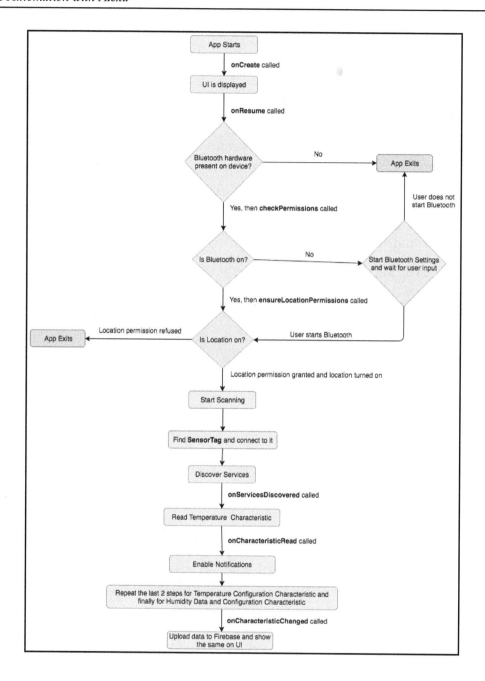

Figure 6.6: Android application flow

Please use the preceding flowchart as a guiding tool while implementing/reviewing your application code implemented in this section. It will give you a bird's-eye view of the code that we are about to implement.

Let's start:

1. Define the user interface to display the current temperature and humidity values on the screen. To do this, we define our UI by updating the `activity_main.xml` file. Remove whatever code is present in this file and you can either add the following code directly to the `activity_main.xml` file or add the UI via the UI editor:

```xml
<?xml version="1.0" encoding="utf-8"?>
<android.support.constraint.ConstraintLayout
xmlns:android="http://schemas.android.com/apk/res/android"
 xmlns:app="http://schemas.android.com/apk/res-auto"
 xmlns:tools="http://schemas.android.com/tools"
 android:layout_width="match_parent"
 android:layout_height="match_parent"
tools:context="android.packt.com.androidwarehousemonitor.MainAc
tivity">
<TextView
  android:id="@+id/textView"
  android:layout_width="0dp"
  android:layout_height="217dp"
  android:layout_marginEnd="8dp"
  android:layout_marginLeft="8dp"
  android:layout_marginRight="8dp"
  android:layout_marginStart="8dp"
  android:layout_marginTop="8dp"
  android:text="Temperature:"
  android:textAppearance="@style/TextAppearance.AppCompat.Large"
  app:layout_constraintHorizontal_bias="0.526"
  app:layout_constraintLeft_toLeftOf="parent"
  app:layout_constraintRight_toRightOf="parent"
  app:layout_constraintTop_toTopOf="parent" />
<TextView
  android:id="@+id/textView2"
  android:layout_width="match_parent"
  android:layout_height="219dp"
  android:layout_marginBottom="8dp"
  android:layout_marginLeft="8dp"
  android:layout_marginRight="8dp"
  android:layout_marginTop="8dp"
  android:text="Humidity:"
  android:textAppearance="@style/TextAppearance.AppCompat.Large"
```

```
app:layout_constraintBottom_toBottomOf="parent"
app:layout_constraintLeft_toLeftOf="parent"
app:layout_constraintRight_toRightOf="parent"
app:layout_constraintTop_toBottomOf="@+id/textView" />
</android.support.constraint.ConstraintLayout>
```

Adding and executing the preceding code should result in the following UI:

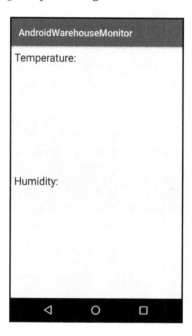

Figure 6.7: Temperature and humidity data UI for the corresponding mobile app

If you ran the app and were able to see the preceding UI, congratulations, you just completed the simple UI layer of the app.

2. Since our UI is ready, we will now move on to add the code, which will enable our app to request for **Bluetooth** and **Location** permissions, which are mandatory for BLE communications.

 To learn more about the Android permissions model, navigate to `https:/ /developer.android.com/guide/topics/permissions/overview`.

For this, add the `ensureLocationPermissionIsEnabled` method to the `MainActivity` class, as follows:

```
private void ensureLocationPermissionIsEnabled() {
  if (Build.VERSION.SDK_INT >= 23 &&
ContextCompat.checkSelfPermission(this,
  android.Manifest.permission.ACCESS_COARSE_LOCATION) !=
PackageManager.PERMISSION_GRANTED) {
  ActivityCompat.requestPermissions(this, new String[]{
  android.Manifest.permission.ACCESS_COARSE_LOCATION},
REQUEST_LOCATION);
  return;
  }
  }
```

After adding the preceding code and compiling the project, you will get an error regarding `REQUEST_LOCATION` not being found. For that error to go away, add the following member variable to the `MainActivity` class:

```
private static final int REQUEST_LOCATION = 1;
```

The `ensureLocationPermissionIsEnabled` method checks whether the location permission is granted, and if not, it requests the permission from the system.

Note that Android Marshmallow (API Level 23) introduced the runtime permission model, which allows the apps to request user permissions in Android at runtime, rather than at compile time, which is also the reason why we check for API Level in the preceding code before requesting runtime permissions. To read more about the runtime permission model, visit `https://developer.android.com/training/permissions/requesting.html`.

The preceding method uses the `ActivityCompat` class, which does all the hard work for us all in a single line of code.

3. The `ActivityCompat` class also provides the `callback` method, which gets called with the user's selection result (whether or not the user granted the permission). Depending on the result, we can take appropriate action. We will also implement this `callback` method, which is called `onRequestPermissionResult`, to listen for results of the permission request presented to the user. Add the following method to your `MainActivity` class:

```
@Override
public void onRequestPermissionsResult(int requestCode,
                                       String permissions[],
    int[] grantResults) {
    switch (requestCode) {
        case REQUEST_LOCATION: {
            // If request is cancelled, the result arrays are
    empty.
            if (grantResults.length > 0
                    && grantResults[0] ==
PackageManager.PERMISSION_GRANTED) {
                Log.i(TAG, "Permission Granted");
            } else {
                Toast.makeText(getApplicationContext(),
                        "Location Permission Not granted",
Toast.LENGTH_LONG).show();
                finish();
            }
            break;
        }
        default:
    }
}
```

The preceding method simply logs it to the console if the permission has been granted; otherwise, it finishes the activity and exits the app. We have added the necessary methods, now we need to call them too.

4. For calling the methods that we added in *Step 2* regarding enabling of location permissions, add a `checkPermissions` method to the `MainActivity` class:

```
private void checkPermissions(BluetoothAdapter
bluetoothAdapter) {
  if (!bluetoothAdapter.isEnabled()) {
  Intent enableBtIntent = new
Intent(BluetoothAdapter.ACTION_REQUEST_ENABLE);
  startActivityForResult(enableBtIntent, REQUEST_ENABLE_BT);
  return;
  }
```

```
ensureLocationPermissionIsEnabled();
}
```

For the code to compile successfully, define the following member variable in the `MainActivity` class:

```
private static final int REQUEST_ENABLE_BT = 0;
```

The preceding `checkPermissions` method will be responsible for enabling Bluetooth and location permissions.

5. In the previous step, we started the **System Default** setting activity for the user and let the user decide whether they wanted to switch the Bluetooth on. However, we are interested in knowing the user's decision, for which we override the `onActivityResult` method in the `MainActivity` class:

```
@Override
protected void onActivityResult(int requestCode, int
resultCode, Intent data) {
  if (requestCode == REQUEST_ENABLE_BT && resultCode == -1) {
   ensureLocationPermissionIsEnabled();
   return;
  }
  Toast.makeText(this, "Bluetooth not turned on",
Toast.LENGTH_LONG).show();
  finish();
}
```

The result of the user's choice (whether the user decided to turn on the Bluetooth or not) will be returned in this method. We finish the activity directly if the user does not turn on the Bluetooth since there isn't much left to do.

6. Let's handle another case, where a device might not have Bluetooth support at all. For that, please update the `onResume` method to the one shown as follows:

```
@Override
    protected void onResume() {
        super.onResume();
        BluetoothManager btManager = (BluetoothManager)
getSystemService(BLUETOOTH_SERVICE);
        BluetoothAdapter btAdapter = btManager != null ?
btManager.getAdapter() : null;
        if (btAdapter == null) {
            Toast.makeText(getApplicationContext(),
                "No Bluetooth Support found",
Toast.LENGTH_LONG).show();
```

```
                finish();
                return;
        }
        checkPermissions(btAdapter);
    }
```

The onResume method in the MainActivity class first checks whether there is Bluetooth support available on the device itself and, if not, finishes the activity. However, if Bluetooth support is found, then it checks for other permissions.

7. We are almost done with the implementation of our new way of requesting and handling **Bluetooth** and **Location** permissions. However, do remember to add the necessary permissions–**Access Coarse Location**, **Bluetooth**, **Bluetooth Admin**, and the internet to the Android Manifest, otherwise our app will not work as expected.

 To read more about permissions related to BLE on the Android platform, visit https://developer.android.com/guide/topics/connectivity/bluetooth-le.html#setup.

Locate the AndroidManifest.xml file (which can be found under the **Manifests** folder located in the root/near the top of the **Project**) in the project explorer of Android Studio, and add the following lines to AndroidManifest.xml directly inside the <manifest> tag:

```
<uses-permission    android:name="android.permission.BLUETOOTH"
/>
<uses-permission
android:name="android.permission.BLUETOOTH_ADMIN"/>
<uses-permission    android:name=
"android.permission.ACCESS_COARSE_LOCATION" />
<uses-permission    android:name=
"android.permission.ACCESS_FINE_LOCATION" />
```

8. We are making an assumption here, that is, the App will be operated in a scenario where the SensorTag (attached to warehouse shelves) is turned on and is always sending out advertisements over Bluetooth Low Energy, so as soon as the app begins its operation, it tries to filter out the SensorTag from the list of broadcasting devices, connect to it, and read temperature and humidity data continuously. For this, add the `startScanning` method to the `MainActivity` class:

```
protected void startScanning() {
        bluetoothManager =
(BluetoothManager)getSystemService(Context.BLUETOOTH_SERVICE);
        bluetoothAdapter = bluetoothManager.getAdapter();
        bluetoothLeScanner =
bluetoothAdapter.getBluetoothLeScanner();
        AsyncTask.execute(new Runnable() { @Override public
void run() { bluetoothLeScanner.startScan(leScanCallback); }
});
    }
```

The `startScanning` method makes use of quite a few variables, so declare those in the `MainActivity` class:

```
BluetoothManager bluetoothManager;
BluetoothAdapter bluetoothAdapter;
BluetoothLeScanner bluetoothLeScanner;
```

We now need to call the `startScanning` method from two places, first, immediately after the user grants the location permission. For this, add the method call to the `startScanning` method to the `onRequestPermissionResult` method (which we implemented in *Step 3*) as shown next:

```
if (grantResults.length > 0 && grantResults[0] ==
PackageManager.PERMISSION_GRANTED) {
  Log.i(TAG, "Permission Granted");
  startScanning();
  }
```

Second, if you have already granted all the permissions during the initial run of the app, we also add the method call for the `startScanning` method to the `ensureLocationPermissionIsEnabled` method (which we implemented in *Step 2*):

```
private void ensureLocationPermissionIsEnabled() {
        if (Build.VERSION.SDK_INT >= 23 &&
```

```
ContextCompat.checkSelfPermission(this,
            android.Manifest.permission.ACCESS_COARSE_LOCATION)
!= PackageManager.PERMISSION_GRANTED) {
        ActivityCompat.requestPermissions(this, new String[]{
android.Manifest.permission.ACCESS_COARSE_LOCATION},
REQUEST_LOCATION);
        return;
    }
    startScanning();
}
```

We have implemented our device scan code. Now, we need to define a callback that handles the devices found.

9. If you were able to accomplish the previous step successfully, your implementation of the startScanning method will make use of ScanCallback, where the results of the scan get delivered. Please define ScanCallback in the MainActivity class:

```
// Device scan callback.
private ScanCallback leScanCallback = new ScanCallback() {
    @Override
    public void onScanResult(int callbackType, ScanResult
result) {
        if (result.getDevice() != null) {
            if (result.getDevice().getName() != null &&
result.getDevice().getName().contains(NAME_TAG)) {
                Log.i(TAG, result.getDevice().getName());
                if (connected == false) {
                    connected = true;
bluetoothLeScanner.stopScan(leScanCallback);
result.getDevice().connectGatt(MainActivity.this, true,
gattCallback);
                }
            }
        }
    }
};
```

Examine the preceding piece of code closely, which is filtering available devices on the basis of names of the devices found. The previously mentioned piece of code uses a few variables, which need to be declared in the MainActivity class:

```
private static String NAME_TAG = "SensorTag";
private boolean connected = false;
```

We will need to match the name of each device found with the name of the
`SensorTag`, and the `NAME_TAG` variable will help us do exactly that. Once the
correct match is found, we initiate a connection by calling the `connectGatt`
method and indicate that the connection request has been made by updating the
state of the `connected` variable.

10. The call to the `connectGatt` method takes three arguments. The last argument is
    a `callback` method, which can be used for:
    - Monitoring connection-state changes
    - Service discovery
    - Characteristic changes

    We will initially implement this callback in the `MainActivity` class for listening
    to connection-state changes:

    ```
    protected BluetoothGattCallback gattCallback = new
    BluetoothGattCallback() {
        @Override
        public void onConnectionStateChange(BluetoothGatt gatt, int
    status, int newState) {
            super.onConnectionStateChange(gatt, status, newState);
            if (newState == BluetoothGatt.STATE_CONNECTED) {
                Log.i(TAG, "onConnectionStateChange() -
    STATE_CONNECTED");
                gatt.discoverServices();
            }
        }
    };
    ```

    As per the preceding implementation, if the connection succeeds, then we initiate
    service discovery.

11. We are interested in two services: `IR_TEMPERATURE_SERVICE` and
    `HUMIDITY_SERVICE`. We first define their UUID(s) in the `MainActivity` class:

    ```
    private static final String UUID_IR_TEMPERATURE_SERVICE =
    "f000aa00-0451-4000-b000-000000000000";
    private static final String UUID_HUMIDITY_SERVICE =
    "f000aa20-0451-4000-b000-000000000000";
    ```

Please note that although we define the UUIDs for both `TEMPERATURE_SERVICE` and `HUMIDITY_SERVICE`, we only demonstrate reading data from `TEMPERATURE_SERVICE` in the Android code sample. Reading data from `HUMIDITY_SERVICE` is similar and is left for you to do as an exercise. Going forward, we will focus specifically on the details of `TEMPERATURE_SERVICE`.

`TEMPERATURE_SERVICE` on the SensorTag consists of two important characteristics: the *data characteristic* and the *configuration characteristic*.

Visit the following link to get insights regarding characteristics exposed by the SensorTag Temperature Service: `http://processors.wiki.ti.com/images/a/a8/BLE_SensorTag_GATT_Server.pdf`.

As the name suggests, the data characteristic holds the temperature data and supports *reading* that data and *enabling/disabling notifications* for the temperature data. We will be interacting with both of these characteristics. Define them in the `MainActivity` class:

```
//Characteristic UUIDs
private static final UUID UUID_CHARACTERISTIC_TEMPERATURE_DATA
= UUID.fromString("f000aa01-0451-4000-b000-000000000000");
private static final UUID
UUID_CHARACTERISTIC_TEMPERATURE_CONFIG =
UUID.fromString("f000aa02-0451-4000-b000-000000000000");
```

Our results of service discovery, which we initiated in the last step, will be delivered in the `onServicesDiscovered` method. Override the `onServicesDiscovered` method as a part of `BluetoothGattCallback`:

```
@Override
public void onServicesDiscovered(final BluetoothGatt gatt, int
status) {
  super.onServicesDiscovered(gatt, status);
gatt.readCharacteristic(gatt.getService(UUID_IR_TEMPERATURE_SER
VICE).getCharacteristic(UUID_CHARACTERISTIC_TEMPERATURE_DATA));
}
```

Once the service discovery is finished, we instruct `BluetoothGatt` to read the temperature data characteristic through the preceding code mentioned.

12. As already pointed out, the temperature data characteristic supports notifications, and we can enable these notifications for periodic data updates for temperature data. Once we have successfully read the temperature data characteristic, we can enable notifications for this characteristic while overriding the onCharacteristicRead method in the BluetoothGattCallback implementation:

```
@Override
public void onCharacteristicRead(BluetoothGatt gatt,
BluetoothGattCharacteristic characteristic, int status) {
 super.onCharacteristicRead(gatt, characteristic, status);
 if
(characteristic.getUuid().equals(UUID_CHARACTERISTIC_TEMPERATUR
E_DATA)) {
   //Enable local notifications
   gatt.setCharacteristicNotification(characteristic, true);
   //Enabled remote notifications
   BluetoothGattDescriptor desc =
characteristic.getDescriptor(CONFIG_DESCRIPTOR);
   desc.setValue(BluetoothGattDescriptor.ENABLE_NOTIFICATION_VALUE
);
   gatt.writeDescriptor(desc);
 }
}
```

Once **Notifications** are enabled, whenever the temperature data is updated on the SensorTag, the app will receive the updated value in the onCharacteristicChanged method.

13. As already pointed out in the last step, we will override the onCharacteristicChanged method so that we can receive the updated temperature value in order to parse and print it on the console:

```
@Override
public void onCharacteristicChanged(BluetoothGatt gatt,
BluetoothGattCharacteristic characteristic) {
 super.onCharacteristicChanged(gatt, characteristic);
 if
(characteristic.getUuid().equals(UUID_CHARACTERISTIC_TEMPERATUR
E_DATA)) {
   double ambient =
Utilities.extractAmbientTemperature(characteristic);
 }
}
```

The temperature data is in the following format:
`ObjectLSB:ObjectMSB:AmbientLSB:AmbientMSB,`. For extracting the data, we have created a separate class called `Utilities`. Add a separate `Utilities` class to the project and introduce the following `extractAmbientTemperature` method in it:

```
public static double
extractAmbientTemperature(BluetoothGattCharacteristic c) {
        int offset = 2;
        return shortUnsignedAtOffset(c, offset) / 128.0;
}
```

The `extractAmbientTemperature` method makes use of the `shortSignedAtOffset` method, hence we will also add that to the `Utilities` class:

```
/**
 * Gyroscope, Magnetometer, Barometer, IR temperature
 * all store 16 bit two's complement values in the awkward
format
 * LSB MSB, which cannot be directly parsed as
getIntValue(FORMAT_SINT16, offset)
 * because the bytes are stored in the "wrong" direction.
 *
 * This function extracts these 16 bit two's complement values.
 * */
private static Integer
shortSignedAtOffset(BluetoothGattCharacteristic c, int offset)
{
 Integer lowerByte = c.getIntValue(FORMAT_UINT8, offset);
 Integer upperByte =
c.getIntValue(BluetoothGattCharacteristic.FORMAT_SINT8, offset
+ 1); // Note: interpret MSB as signed.
 return (upperByte << 8) + lowerByte;
}
```

The preceding code snippet has been sourced from `http://processors.wiki.ti.com/`.

We have enabled **Notifications** for the data characteristic and, theoretically, we should be able to sit back and just wait for the temperature sensor to read, update, and notify the latest temperature values to us via the onCharacteristicChanged method. However, this is not the case, as we are still missing a key step before we can get temperature updates successfully.

14. If you were able to go over the documentation link, which we pointed out in *Step 11*, there is a key detail mentioned in that document:

0x29	41	0xAA02	IR Temperature Config	00	RW	Write "01" to start Sensor and Measurements, "00" to put to sleep

Figure 6.8: Details of the temperature-configuration characteristic

As per the preceding details, please note that by default, the temperature sensor is not enabled to record measurements. Hence, by default, our temperature sensor is in sleep mode; we need to bring it to active mode so that we can receive periodic notifications. We do so by overriding the onDescriptorWrite method in the BluetoothGattCallback implementation in the MainActivity class:

```
@Override
public void onDescriptorWrite(BluetoothGatt gatt,
BluetoothGattDescriptor descriptor, int status) {
    super.onDescriptorWrite(gatt, descriptor, status);
    enableConfigurationForCharacteristic(gatt,
descriptor.getCharacteristic());
}
```

As per the implementation of onDescriptorWrite, we will also need to implement the enableConfigurationForCharacteristic method in the MainActivity class:

```
private void enableConfigurationForCharacteristic(BluetoothGatt
gatt, BluetoothGattCharacteristic characteristic) {
 if
(characteristic.getUuid().equals(UUID_CHARACTERISTIC_TEMPERATUR
E_DATA)) {
gatt.readCharacteristic(gatt.getService(UUID_IR_TEMPERATURE_SER
VICE).getCharacteristic(UUID_CHARACTERISTIC_TEMPERATURE_CONFIG)
);
 }
}
```

This is where the second important characteristic, the configuration characteristic, which we mentioned earlier, comes into play.

15. Following up from the last step, we'll read the configuration characteristic (and update it as a next step) so that we can eventually configure our temperature sensor to move from sleeping to active mode. For updating the configuration characteristic, update the preimplemented `onCharacteristicRead` method to the following:

```
@Override
public void onCharacteristicRead(BluetoothGatt gatt,
BluetoothGattCharacteristic characteristic, int status) {
  super.onCharacteristicRead(gatt, characteristic, status);
  if
(characteristic.getUuid().equals(UUID_CHARACTERISTIC_TEMPERATUR
E_DATA)) {
    //Enable local notifications
    gatt.setCharacteristicNotification(characteristic, true);
    //Enabled remote notifications
    BluetoothGattDescriptor desc =
characteristic.getDescriptor(CONFIG_DESCRIPTOR);
    desc.setValue(BluetoothGattDescriptor.ENABLE_NOTIFICATION_VALUE
);
    gatt.writeDescriptor(desc);
  } else if
(characteristic.getUuid().equals(UUID_CHARACTERISTIC_TEMPERATUR
E_CONFIG)) {
    characteristic.setValue(new byte[] {0x01});
    gatt.writeCharacteristic(characteristic);
  }
}
```

After the successful read, we write `0x01` to the configuration characteristic so that our temperature sensor is set to active mode.

16. We are done with our implementation and now the
    onCharacteristicChanged method should be called for every temperature
    value update on the SensorTag. As a final step, we can update the
    onCharacteristicChanged method to display live temperature updates to the
    user. Also, we can set up and include the data upload to the Firebase backend so
    that our app can keep uploading periodic data updates to the remote server. Our
    final code for the UI updates and upload to the backend is as follows:

```
@Override
public void onCharacteristicChanged(BluetoothGatt gatt,
BluetoothGattCharacteristic characteristic) {
  super.onCharacteristicChanged(gatt, characteristic);
  if
(characteristic.getUuid().equals(UUID_CHARACTERISTIC_TEMPERATUR
E_DATA)) {
    final double ambient =
Utilities.extractAmbientTemperature(characteristic);
    //Upload to Firebase Backend
    FirebaseDatabase database = FirebaseDatabase.getInstance();
    DatabaseReference myRef =
database.getReference("Temperature");
    myRef.setValue(ambient);
    //Update the UI
    runOnUiThread(new Runnable() {
     @Override
     public void run() {
       ((TextView)
findViewById(R.id.textView)).setText("Temperature: " + ambient
+ "\u00b0" + "C");
     }
    });
  }
}
```

Please note that we still need to set up Firebase on both the client and server sides, due to
which the preceding code may fail to compile, as we are referring to Firebase but have not
yet set it up. We will set it up in the next step.

Setting up Firebase

We now have the data, and all that remains is to upload it to a server so that it can be remotely accessible to Alexa as it will need to read/access it. For this, we will integrate Firebase into our Android app and upload the temperature measurement to the Firebase Cloud. We will integrate Firebase into our mobile app by walking through the following steps:

1. To integrate Firebase, in the Android Studio, on the top **Menu** bar, navigate to **Tools** | **Firebase**. This should bring up the Firebase **Assistant** window:

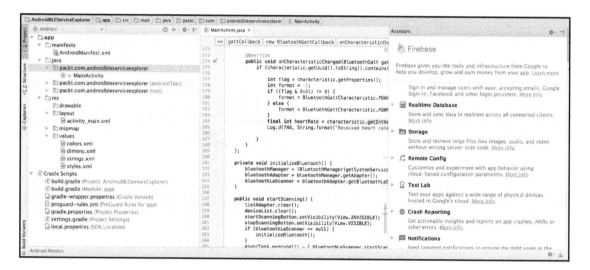

Figure 6.9: Firebase Assistant

2. Under the Firebase **Assistant** window, navigate to **Realtime Database** | **Save and retrieve data**. This should bring up the Save and retrieve data window.

3. Click on **Connect your app to Firebase**. The Firebase connection should ask you to choose an existing project or create a new one.

4. Choose to create a new one, provide it with a relevant name, and click on **Connect to Firebase**:

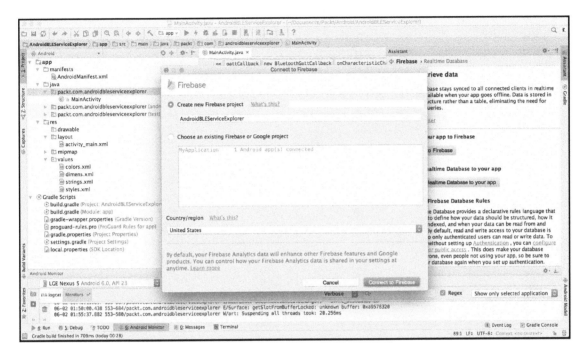

Figure 6.10: Creating a new Firebase project

5. The process will take a few minutes and, on successful completion, the following **Connect your app to Firebase** indicator in the **Assistant** window will turn green:

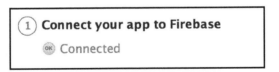

Figure 6.11: Firebase app connection status

6. Click on the second item in the **Assistant** window, which says **Add the Realtime Database to your app**. A prompt comes up, which is essentially asking whether necessary changes regarding the inclusion of Firebase can be made to the project. Click on **Accept Changes** in this prompt:

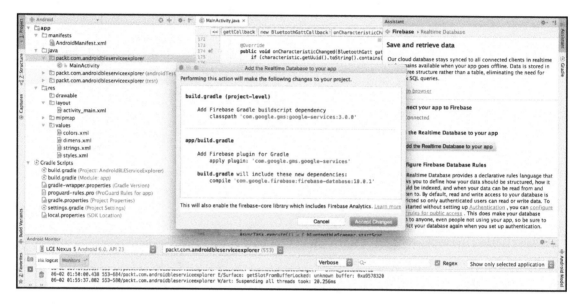

Figure 6.12: Adding Firebase to the project

7. After accepting the changes, a Gradle Sync will start.

8. Post the Gradle Sync, and click on **Configure your rules for public access** under *Step 3* in the assistant window. This step will open the browser with some Firebase documentation.

9. Click on **Go to Console** on the top-right corner of this screen. This should open up a dashboard/gallery of existing applications.

10. Choose a relevant application name:

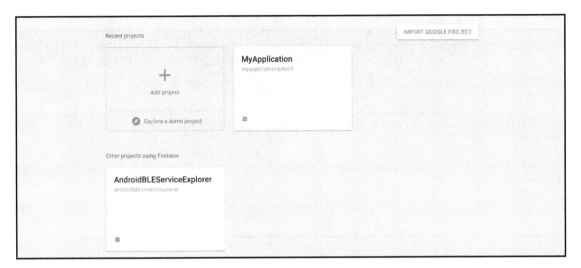

Figure 6.13: Firebase apps console

11. You should be taken to a details console. From here, click on **Database** in the left pane and select the **Rules** tab from the list of horizontal tabs.
12. What you should be seeing in front of you is a JSON file signifying rules as key-value pairs:
    1. Change the .read key from `auth != null` to `true`.
    2. Do the same for the .write key.
    3. Hit the **Publish** button at the top.

This configuration is for demo purposes only, which means anyone can read or write to your database. In the real world, your rules will be more advanced and sophisticated than this.

The security rules JSON should look like the one shown as follows when you have done the above-mentioned changes:

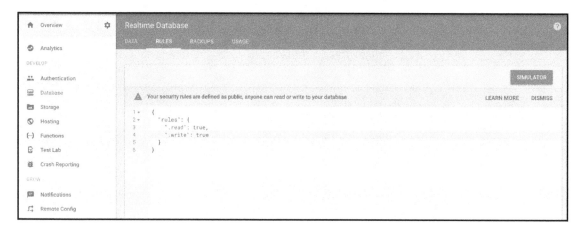

Figure 6.14: Firebase detailed console and rules

13. Once you have made these changes, our Android app already has the code to upload the readings to the Firebase backend. If you launch the app now, turn on the SensorTag, and keep it advertising near the app, you should see dynamic temperature updates coming in and the UI getting updated:

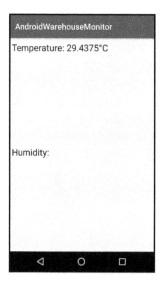

Figure 6.15: Dynamic temperature updates

Phew, that was something! And we are done with our Android implementation.

 Please note that if you run the app and are not able to see the devices getting discovered (in the logs or while debugging), make sure that your phone has location services switched on.

You should also be able to see the live updates on the Firebase backend, which match the data being shown on the app:

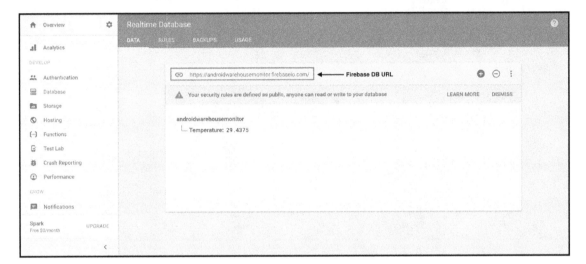

Figure 6.16: Dynamic updates to Firebase

Copy the Firebase DB URL (it may be different in your case, depending on how you named your Firebase db) and save it somewhere. We will need to reference it from the Lambda code.

 You can find the code for `AndroidWarehouseMonitor` at `https://github.com/madhurbhargava/AndroidWarehouseMonitor`.

We will now go ahead and implement the actual Ambience Manager Skill.

Developing the Ambience Manager Skill

As always, we will be making use of the Alexa Skills Kit (ASK) Console to configure the Ambience Manager Skill:

1. Navigate to `https://developer.amazon.com/alexa`, and click on the **Sign In** button located in the top-right corner of the screen:

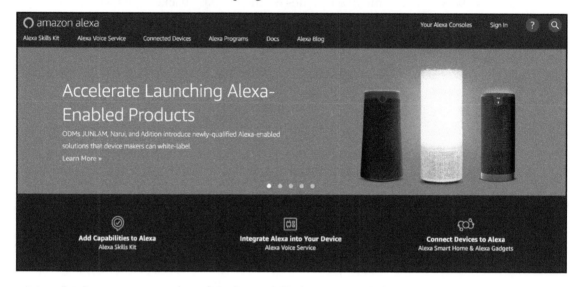

Figure 6.17: Alexa Skills portal

2. After signing in, click on the **Alexa Skills Kit** menu item on the top-left, and from the menu, select **Get Started | Alexa Skills Kit**:

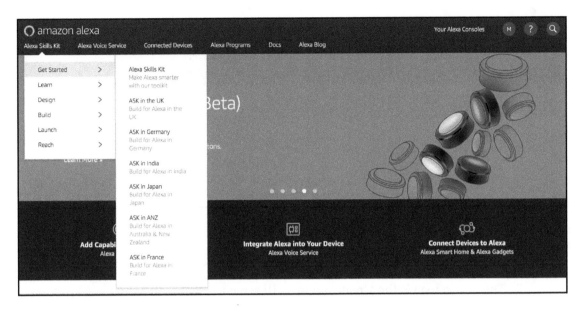

Figure 6.18: Alexa Skills Portal – signing in

3. On the screen that appears next, click on the **Start a Skill** button, located in the center of the screen:

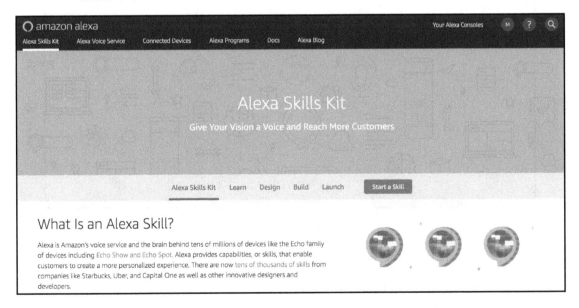

Figure 6.19: Alexa Skills Portal – starting a skill

4. This should land you on the ASK Console:

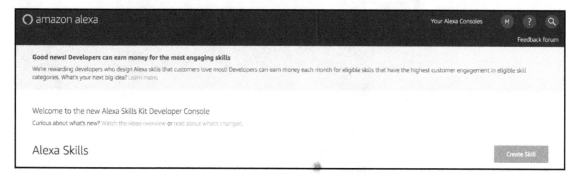

Figure 6.20: Alexa Skills Portal – ASK Console

Click on the **Create Skill** button located at the bottom of the screen.

5. The next screen is the **Create a new skill** screen, which will require a **SkillName** to proceed further:

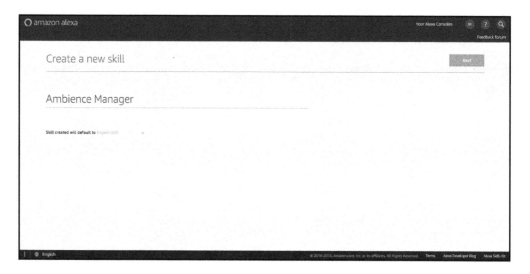

Figure 6.21: Naming the skill

Please name the skill `Ambience Manager` and click on the **Next** button.

6. The next page will display the type of prebuilt interaction models that can be added to the skill:

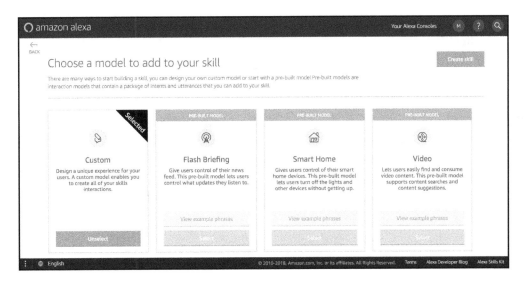

Figure 6.22: Choosing a Custom interaction model for the skill

Click on the **Select** button under the **Custom** model to select it, and click on the **Create skill** button in the top-right corner of the screen.

7. After skill creation, we will need to configure its **Interaction Model** via the dashboard:

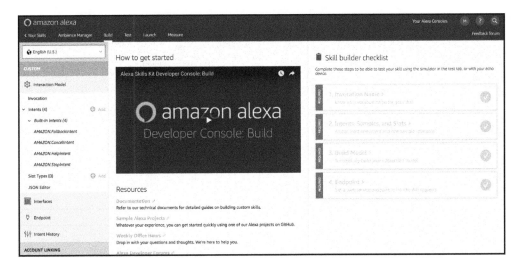

Figure 6.23: Ambience Manager Skill dashboard

We will configure the **Interaction Model** by completing the **Skill builder checklist**.

8. Select the first option, **Invocation Name**, under the **Skill builder checklist** to land on the following screen:

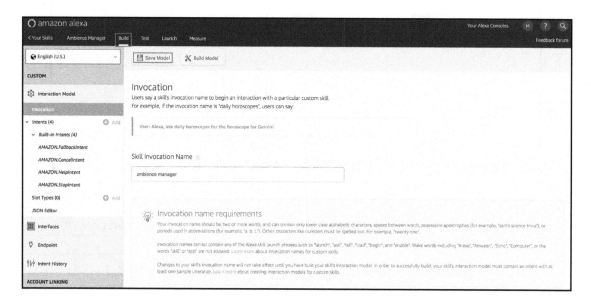

Figure 6.24: Providing an Invocation Name

Enter the **Skill Invocation Name** as `ambience manager` and click on the **Save Model** button in the top-left corner.

9. Click on the **Build** tab item to end up on the **Skill builder checklist**, which should have the **Invocation Name** option marked and selected since we just completed setting it up:

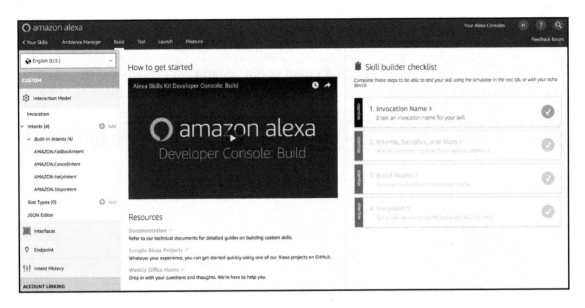

Figure 6.25: Setting up Intents, Samples, and Slots after setting up Invocation Name

Now, as our **Invocation Name** is set up, please select the **Intents, Samples, and Slots** item from the checklist to land on the **Add Intent** screen:

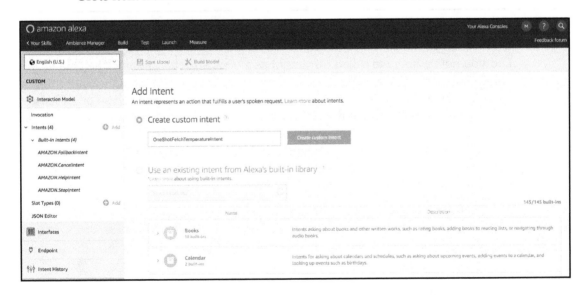

Figure 6.26: Creating the One-Shot Intent

Name the intent `OneShotFetchTemperatureIntent` and click on the **Create custom intent** button.

10. Clicking on the **Create custom intent** button should land you on the **Sample Utterances** page for the `OneShotFetchTemperatureIntent` intent:

Figure 6.27: Configuring the One-Shot Intent

Did you notice how we called our intent as a `One Shot...` intent. The One-Shot intents are different than regular intents due to the fact that One-Shot intents launch your skill and ask it to do some work (fetch some data, and so on). Please note that the naming convention of starting the name of the intent with `OneShot...` is *not* mandatory and you can name it what you like, however it is a good practice that the intent name reflects its purpose. One-Shot intents are simply a different way of launching a skill. You will also notice this difference when we write our Lambda code.

 To read more about One-Shot Intent/Launch, navigate to `https://developer.amazon.com/docs/custom-skills/voice-interface-and-user-experience-testing-for-a-custom-skill.html`.

We can now add a few utterances for our model, as shown in the following screenshot:

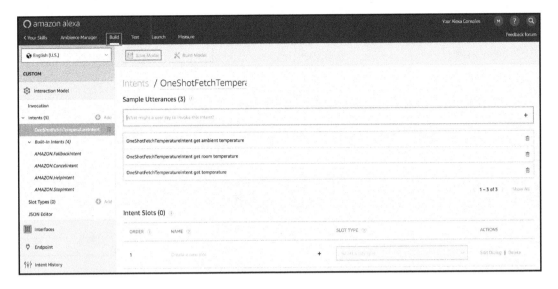

Figure 6.28: Adding Sample Utterances for the One-Shot Intent

Please click on the **Save Model** button after configuring the utterances.

11. Once you have finished setting up the utterances, select the **Build** tab (as seen in *Figure 6.28*) to land on the dashboard:

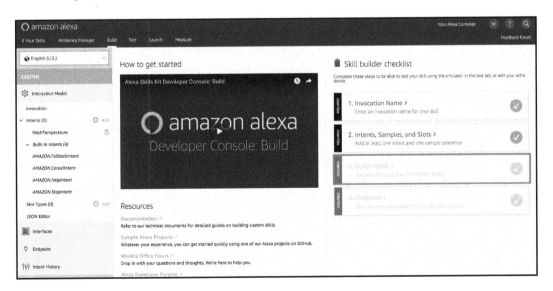

Figure 6.29: Building the Model

Finally, select the **Build Model** option to build the **Interaction Model**. The process should take a few minutes. The **Build Model** button on the dashboard should turn green after the build finishes successfully.

12. After the **Interaction Model** has finished building, we now need to supply it with a Lambda endpoint to connect to. We will postpone this step for a little bit while we code our Lambda. But before we start configuring the Lambda, click on the **Endpoint** button on the dashboard shown in the preceding screenshot to navigate to the **Endpoint** screen:

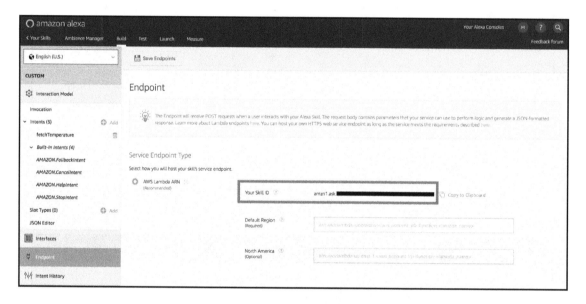

Figure 6.30: Copying the ARN endpoint

Select **AWS Lambda ARN** from the given options, and copy the Skill ID from this page and save it somewhere. We will need it shortly.

Configuring the Lambda function

Once the **Interaction Model** is created, we will leave the Configuration Dashboard as it is and focus on creating the Lambda:

1. Open a new browser tab and navigate to the AWS console.

> The AWS console can be found at `https://console.aws.amazon.com`. Please note that you may need to create a new account if you do not already have one.

Select **Lambda** under **Services | Compute** options. Click **Create a function** on the next screen, name the Lambda function `ambienceManagerSkill`, and fill in the details as shown in the following screenshot:

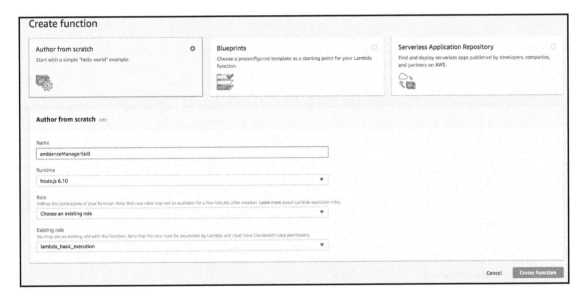

Figure 6.31: Setting up the Lambda function

Click on the **Create function** button after filling in the details.

2. On the next screen, under the **Designer** section, you will need to add a trigger to invoke the Lambda function. From the list of triggers on the left, please select **Alexa Skills Kit** since Alexa will be invoking and supplying input to our Lambda function:

Figure 6.32: Adding the trigger to the Lambda function

Once we have added the trigger, we need to add the Skill ID that we copied in the previous section. Scroll to the bottom of the screen and add the **Skill ID** in the section shown in the following screenshot:

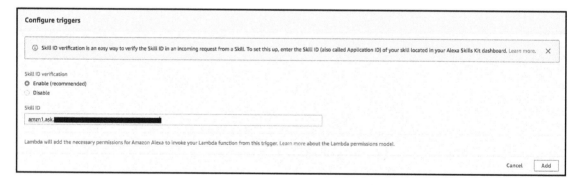

Figure 6.33: Configuring the trigger

Adding the **Skill ID** ensures that the Lambda responds to only those requests that are generated by the verified skill. After adding the **Skill ID**, please click on the **Add** button at the bottom of the screen. Our Lambda configuration should have some unsaved changes now. Please save the recent changes by clicking on **Save** button in the top-right corner of the screen.

3. Once you have clicked the **Save** button, select the **ambienceManagerSkill** box under the **Designer** section. This should bring up a code editor at the bottom where we will add the code for the Lambda.

Coding the Lambda function

Following the Lambda setup, it's time to code the actual Lambda function. We will be editing the code inline, in the `index.js` file on the Developer Portal itself, following these steps:

1. Implement the handling of events in `exports.handler`. Our Lambda, in this case, will be handling only a single intent, that is, `OneShotFetchTemperatureIntent`. Since we are implementing a One-Shot Launch, this single intent will launch our skill and fetch the temperature data.

   Before we move on to write the functional logic, declare the following variables, which will be used by our functional logic:

   ```
   var https = require('https');
   var firebaseHost = "androidwarehousemonitor.firebaseio.com";
   ```

   `firebaseHost` is the same URL (it may be different in your case, depending on how you set up Firebase for the Android app) that we copied earlier when we were setting up Firebase. Since we will be connecting to Firebase via a REST call, we will need its `firebaseHost` URL and `https`.

   Then, update the code of `exports.handler`, as shown here:

   ```
   exports.handler = (event, context, callback) => {
       try {
           if (event.request.type === "IntentRequest") {
               if ("OneShotFetchTemperatureIntent" ===
   event.request.intent.name) {
               } else {
                   throw "Invalid intent";
               }
           }
   ```

```
    }
    catch(e) {
        context.fail("Exception: " + e);
    }
};
```

As shown and discussed previously, we have discarded all the other intents (even the Launch Intent, which we have handled religiously so far) and handled just `OneShotFetchTemperatureIntent` to facilitate the One-Shot Launch of our skill.

2. We will define some helper functions that will help us create speech responses, shown as follows:

```
// ------- Helper functions -------

function buildSpeechletResponse(output, repromptText,
shouldEndSession) {
    return {
        outputSpeech: {
            type: "PlainText",
            text: output
        },
        reprompt: {
            outputSpeech: {
                type: "PlainText",
                text: repromptText
            }
        },
        shouldEndSession: shouldEndSession
    };
}


function buildResponse(sessionAttributes, speechletResponse) {
    return {
        version: "1.0",
        sessionAttributes: sessionAttributes,
        response: speechletResponse
    };
}
```

These functions help the Lambda to return the response to be spoken by Alexa whenever it receives a specific intent/input.

The `buildResponse` function will generate the plain-spoken response to be spoken by Alexa.

The `buildSpeechletResponse` function will specify the output that Alexa will eventually speak, in the form of plain text. It also takes another variable, `shouldEndSession`, which specifies whether Alexa should end the session after the response.

Define the `fbGet` function, which will take a key parameter and fetch the data from a provided host via a REST call:

```
function fbGet(key){
    return new Promise((resolve, reject) => {
        var options = {
            hostname: firebaseHost,
            port: 443,
            path: key + ".json",
            method: 'GET'
        };
        var req = https.request(options, function (res) {
            res.setEncoding('utf8');
            var body = '';
            res.on('data', function(chunk) {
                body += chunk;
            });
            res.on('end', function() {
                resolve(JSON.parse(body))
            });
        });
        req.end();
        req.on('error', reject);
    });
}
```

The preceding function will take the parameter for the key that holds the temperature data (in our case, that key is *Temperature*) and fetches the data from the Firebase Host. The data is received in JSON format and hence needs to be parsed.

3. Once we have added this method, we will need to call it from `exports.handler`. Update `exports.handler` with the call to `fbGet`, as shown in the following code:

```
exports.handler = (event, context, callback) => {
    try {
        if (event.request.type === "IntentRequest") {
```

```
                if ("OneShotFetchTemperatureIntent" ===
    event.request.intent.name) {
                    fbGet("/Temperature").then(res => {
    context.succeed(buildResponse(buildSpeechletResponse("The
    temperature is . . " + res + " . degrees", true)));
                    })
            } else {
                throw "Invalid intent";
            }
        }
    }
    catch(e) {
        context.fail("Exception: " + e);
    }
};
```

Upon a successful fetch, we create a speech response and pass it back to be spoken by Alexa. This completes our Lambda implementation.

4. We need to link the Lambda to our skill and for this purpose, we will need the **Amazon Resource Number (ARN)** of our Lambda. The ARN is located in the top-right corner of the Lambda function/code editor page:

Figure 6.34: Copying the ARN

Copy the ARN. Once you have copied it, navigate to the previous browser tab where we were configuring the **Interaction Model** of our skill:

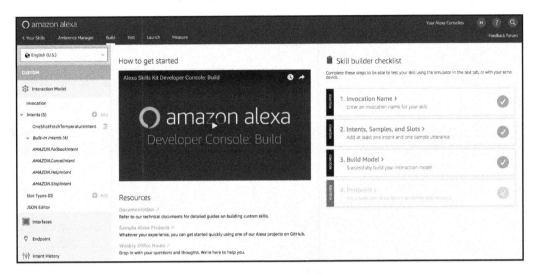

Figure 6.35: Updating the Endpoint with ARN – step 1

As seen in the preceding screenshot, click on the **Endpoint** button under the **Skill builder checklist**, which should navigate you to the **Endpoint** screen, as shown in the following screenshot:

Figure 6.36: Updating the Endpoint with ARN– step 2

Select **AWS Lambda ARN**, under the **Default Region** option, add the ARN that we copied from the previous screen and click on the **Save Endpoints** button in the top-left of the screen.

After clicking on the **Save Endpoints** button, please click on the **Build** tab again to navigate to the dashboard.

5. On the dashboard, all the items on the **Skill builder checklist** should now be green, as shown in the following screenshot:

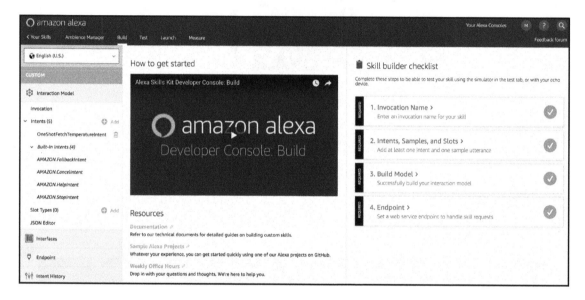

Figure 6.37: Completing the Skill builder checklist

This indicates that our skill is now ready to be tested. Please click on the **Test** tab shown in the preceding screenshot.

Testing and debugging the Skill

The **Test** tab should bring up the Alexa Simulator:

Figure 6.38: Alexa Simulator

Alexa Simulator greatly reduces the need for an actual Amazon Echo since you can easily test the Ambience Manager Skill using just the Simulator.

Please enter `Alexa ask ambience manager to get temperature` in the text box, as shown in the following screenshot, and press *Enter*:

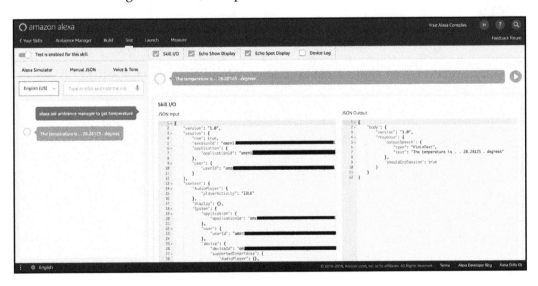

Figure 6.39: Launching the skill via the Skill Simulator

Alexa should reply with the correct response of "*The temperature is....*", and if the volume of your computer is turned on, you can even hear Alexa speaking that response.

Our skill is now tested and ready to be played around with. You can find the code of the Lambda for this chapter at the link mentioned in the information box.

 Please find the code for the Lambda here: `https://github.com/madhurbhargava/AlexaSkillsProjects/blob/master/Chapter_6_Smart_Home_Index.js`.

However, what happens if an error occurs and the skill does not behave the way we wanted it to?

One of the effective debugging tools for an Alexa skill is Amazon CloudWatch. CloudWatch can show you the complete log details of what happens when you launch your skill and how it handles various intents. If you have Log Statements in your Lambda code, you can also check the program flow via the output of those Log Statements in CloudWatch.

CloudWatch can be accessed from the AWS console.

 To access CloudWatch, visit `https://console.aws.amazon.com`.

To check the status of your skill's execution, select **CloudWatch** from the list of **AWS services** on the AWS Console, as shown in the following screenshot:

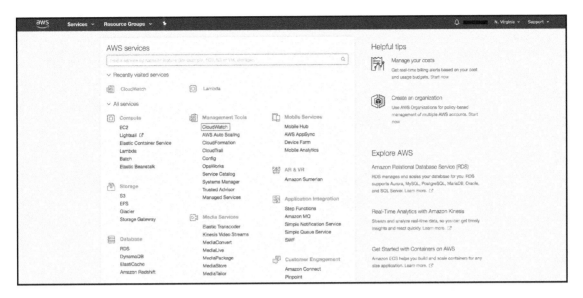

Figure 6.40: Launching CloudWatch

This should land you on the CloudWatch dashboard, shown in the following screenshot, which offers a lot of functionality apart from just the **Logs**:

Figure 6.41: CloudWatch dashboard

However, what we are interested in is the **Logs**, so click on the **Logs** option:

Figure 6.42: Launching Logs from the CloudWatch dashboard

This should show you the list of skills that you have and for which there are logs available. Clicking on the skill of your choice should bring you the list of the available logs, sorted chronologically. You can click on any of those and see the detailed logging with a complete list of events that your skill has responded to:

Figure 6.43: Logs list in CloudWatch

Summary

We hope you enjoyed creating the Ambience Manager Skill. This skill had a lot of moving parts that were not Alexa-specific, such as Firebase, the ambient sensor, and the mobile app. We also covered the One-Shot Launch, and skill debugging via CloudWatch.

As with the previous skills, the Ambience Manager Skill still has room for improvement, such as handling humidity data and the introduction of additional intents.

We have left the improvements as an exercise for the user to hone the skill even further.

We also hope that you are now a little more confident with your knowledge regarding Alexa skills and can't wait to see what you create next.

In the last chapter, we will explore the future of Voice-Based Assistants.

7
The Future of Voice-Based Personal Assistants

"Do or do not. There is no try."

– Master Yoda

We have completed six chapters, during which we have focused solely on Alexa. In this chapter, which is also the last chapter, we will still focus on Alexa and some of its most popular skills, but in comparison with its various competitors. We will also discuss the future of various voice-computing technologies available out there, including Alexa. In this chapter, we will cover the following topics:

- Popular Alexa Skills
- Comparing Various Voice-Based Assistants
- Future of Voice-Based Assistants

We are looking at these topics to consolidate the information that we have covered so far, and to brainstorm how the future of voice computing will look.

Popular Alexa Skills

At the time of writing, the total count of Alexa Skills available in the US, which is also the biggest market for Amazon Alexa, has surpassed 30,000, with an average of 50 new skills getting published each day. Each of these skills is available under a specific category, and the Alexa Skills Store is currently letting the developers and users choose from 23 different major categories, as shown in the following screenshot:

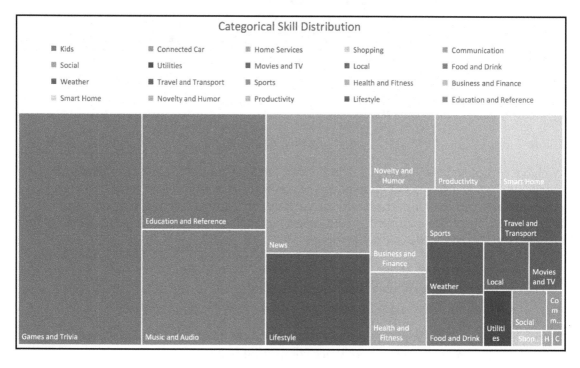

Figure 7.1: Alexa Skills – categorical distribution

At the time of writing (mid-2018), the most popular categories (the ones that have the most skills) among developers are:

- **Games and Trivia**: Hosts over 6,000 skills
- **News**: Hosts over 3,000 skills
- **Music and Audio**: Hosts over 3,000 skills
- **Education and Reference**: Hosts over 3,000 skills
- **Lifestyle**: Hosts over 2,000 skills

Among the top five, the distribution is as follows:

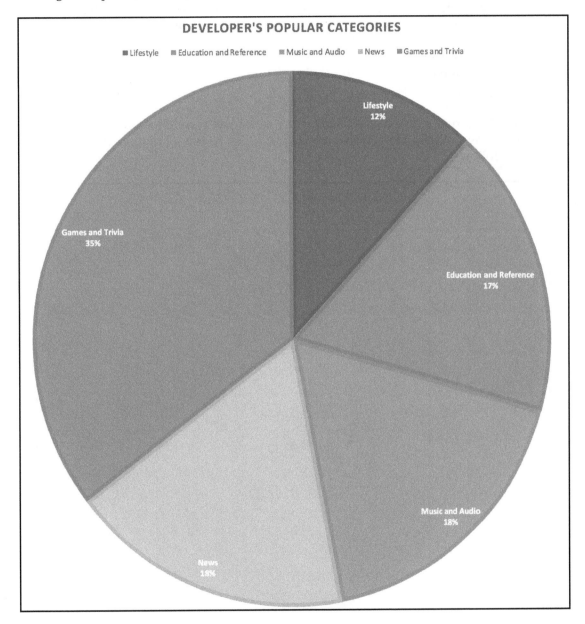

Figure 7.2: Alexa Skills – most popular categories

This should not come as a surprise, since these categories are equally as popular for smartphone apps. However, the difference arises when we go over the list of all 23 available categories (see *Figure 7.1*) and find a few specific categories, such as:

- **Connected Car**: Hosts over 34 skills
- **Smart Home**: Hosts over 972 skills
- **Home Services**: Hosts over 36 skills

These categories are pretty niche and hence have a lot more accommodation room and fewer competing skills. The lowest five categories, which have a lot of room for growth, are depicted as follows:

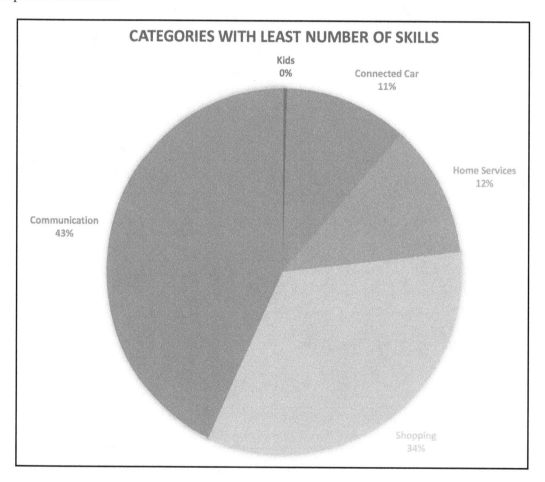

Figure 7.3: Alexa Skills – least popular categories

Surprisingly, at the time of writing, the **Kids** category has the fewest skills, which makes it developers' least favorite category to develop for, but on the bright side, it has the lowest amount of competition and a lot of room for growth.

So far, we have seen the various categories on the Alexa Skills Store and also outlined the most and least popular categories of all the available categories. Now, delving deeper into the categories, let's identify the best of the best, that is, the skills that are most downloaded/used among the top major categories.

Games and Trivia

One of the top downloaded skills under the **Games and Trivia** category is Would You Rather For Family, which has over 3,000 ratings and user reviews.

 To learn more about the Would You Rather For Family Alexa Skill, please visit `https://www.amazon.com/Would-You-Rather-For-Family/dp/B06WGV16HR`.

It is the voice-computed version of the popular game Would You Rather, which has Alexa asking the players tricky/trivial questions and the players replying to those. To keep the fun in the game, new questions are continuously added by the developers.

Other popular skills in this category include Question of the Day, Jeopardy, and Twenty Questions. We suggest that you check them out on the Alexa Skills Store.

News

No surprise here, some of the top news-providing skills are from the channels and media houses that we are already familiar with:

- BBC
- CNN
- ESPN
- Fox News

Some channels even have different options for their skills, depending on the user's requirement. For example, CNN has developed and provided two different skills, one for providing flash briefings and the other for regular news. We suggest that you check them out on the Alexa Skills Store.

Music and Audio

The top *official* skills under this category are for **Ambient Sounds**, which provide Alexa with the capability of playing rain, thunderstorm, and ocean sounds, which can help users relax and sleep better. However, Alexa can also be linked to your Spotify account, if you have one, and can double as an excellent music player.

 To learn more about Spotify and Alexa integration, navigate to `https://www.spotify.com/us/amazonalexa/`.

Hence, Spotify with Alexa is one of the top contenders in this category.

Education and Reference

One of the top downloaded skills under this category is Word of the Day, which has over 900 ratings and promises to teach the user a new word, and how to use it in a sentence, every day.

 To learn more about the Word of the Day skill, visit `https://www.amazon.com/Volley-Inc-Word-the-Day/dp/B06VTHH5MW/`.

As per the developers of the skill, it is updated daily with new content.

Lifestyle

The most popular skills under this category are for **Meditation/Zen Sounds**, which provide Alexa with the capability of playing soothing sounds, which can help the users to meditate.

Another popular skill in this category is **Fitbit**; using this skill, a user can keep track of their details recorded via the Fitbit fitness tracker and fitness goals using Alexa.

We have seen the best skills under the top five categories offered by the Alexa Skills Store. Now, a question to you: did you notice any common traits among the top-selling skills? Take a few minutes to think this over before moving ahead to read the answer.

Well, we hope you have given it some thought by now. Here is the answer: all the top skills in these categories have one common feature—**dynamism**. This means they are updated with new features very frequently, and some are even updated daily. Take any skill (with the exception of the News skills, since their daily content is already dynamic in itself); whether it is a **Games/Trivia** skill or an educational skill, if it is in one of the top spots, then it stays one step ahead of its users by always providing them with something new to discover, which keeps the users hooked to the Skill, and they keep coming back to discover more content. Dynamism of content is the key if you want your skill to be a leader in its category.

We've looked at various categories and Alexa Skills; let's now move on to analyze and compare various voice-based personal assistants.

Comparing Various Voice-Based Assistants

Although we have already discussed and compared various voice-based assistants to some extent in Chapter 1, *What is Alexa?*, in this section we will limit our discussion to voice-enabled speakers that host these assistants.

As of 2018, there are only a few major players in the voice-enabled speaker market (*source: voicebot.ai*), namely Amazon, which holds the lion's share of 52%, then Google Home, standing at 32%, Apple's HomePod at 12%, and the rest of the market is divided between several other players, as depicted in the following pie chart:

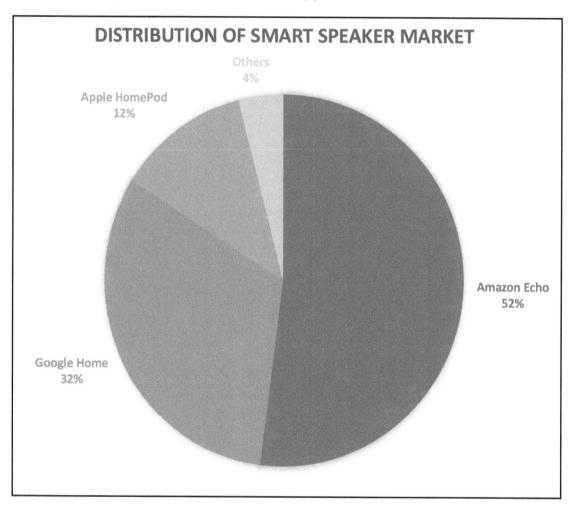

Figure 7.4: Alexa Skills – distribution of smart speaker market

We will cover three of the major players in this section; **Amazon Echo**, **Google Home**, and **Apple HomePod**.

Amazon Echo

Introduced in November 2014, the Echo series of smart speakers by Amazon had the first mover's advantage in the voice-computing market, which enabled it to grab the lion's share of 70% of the complete market. But that is not the only thing going for it; Amazon offers the widest range of voice-enabled speakers, each with its own distinctive usage, some of which are mentioned as follows:

- **Echo Dot**: Smallest and most affordable.
- **Echo**: Mid-range product, slightly better sound quality than Echo Dot.
- **Echo Plus**: Bigger than Echo with best sound quality. Has a Zigbee hub built in for better smart-home integration.
- **Echo Spot**: Circular Echo with a screen.
- **Echo Spot**: Echo with a larger screen, ideal for video chatting.

The wide range of products ensures that there is something for every need and taste. Also, the cheapest Echo product is around $50, which makes it one of the major affordable choices out of the three brands.

The screen-based Echo already adds the video playback functionality to the smart speaker, which is a big add-on. None of the other two major players(Google and Apple) has such a device that has the combined functionality of a smart speaker powered with video playback.

Also, Amazon has already created a skills-based ecosystem for the Echo products, which enables the Echo to seamlessly integrate with various third-party services, such as Uber and Domino's.

Google Home

Introduced in late 2016, Google Home was launched to directly compete against Amazon Echo, with the Google Assistant being Alexa's counterpart. The Google Home devices have a slightly narrower range as compared to the Echo series of devices:

- **Google Home Mini**: Smallest, most affordable, and priced similarly to Echo Dot.
- **Google Home**: Original Google flagship smart speaker. Has better sound quality than Google Home Mini.
- **Google Home Max**: Largest, best sound quality, and most expensive of the three.

All three are powered by the Google Assistant, and so the differentiating points come down to form factors, voice quality, and pricing between the Home Mini, Home, and Home Max:

Figure 7.5: Google Home, Mini, and Max (Source: speakerfanatic.com)

Compared with Amazon Echo, since Google's niche is web search, Google Home is slightly more conversational and better at handling web-based queries. However, Amazon Echo quickly tried to bridge that gap by supporting a larger number of smart home brands than Google Home, which is due to the fact that Amazon, being the first to the market, had already expanded its Skill-based ecosystem to pull in more and more third-party developers. However, we are pretty sure that Google Home will catch up soon, or at least provide some tough competition.

Apple HomePod

Introduced in late 2017 and released in early 2018, HomePod by Apple is an attempt to counterstrike the Amazon Echo and Google Home:

Figure 7.6: Apple HomePod (source: wikimedia.org)

It is a smart speaker by Apple, with Siri being the counterpart to the Google Assistant and Alexa. Priced at $349 (at the time of writing), it is second only to Google Home Max (priced at $399) in terms of price.

HomePod's design provides it with 360-degree sound with good clarity and quality, however, it is tightly coupled with Apple's ecosystem. For example, Amazon Echo and Google Home easily integrate with third-party services, such as Spotify, which is a little difficult on Apple HomePod.

We hope that you now have a good idea of what each smart speaker has to offer, and how they compare to each other. With this information, we'll move to the last section, where we will discuss the future of smart speakers.

Future of Voice-Based Assistants

In the infancy of the smart speaker market in 2016, the total number of smart speaker units sold was less than 10 million, however, at the beginning of the latter half of 2017, Amazon Echo had sold more than 20 million devices alone (source: *voicebot.ai*) and it is predicted (source: *voicebot.ai*) that, during 2018, more than 56 million smart speaker devices will be sold:

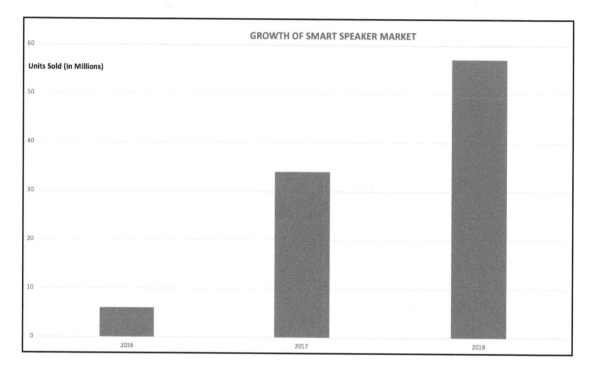

Figure 7.7: Growth of smart speaker market

Also, by 2020, it is predicted (source: *Gartner, Edison Research 2017*) that 75% of US households will have a smart speaker:

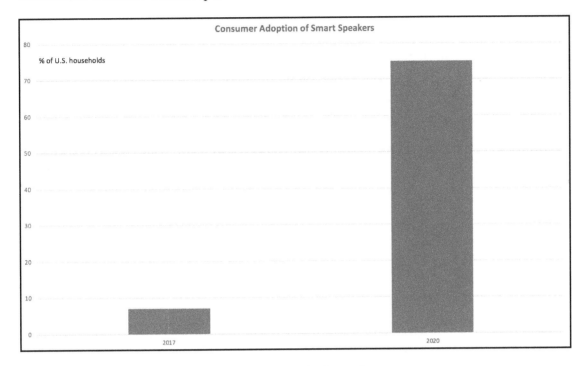

Figure 7.8: Consumer adoption of smart speakers

The preceding statistics predict a market poised to grow exponentially and explode over the coming years. Also, the pitching in of Google and Apple with their own voice-computing devices only consolidates this fact.

No doubt, this is the best time to develop for voice since the technology, the hardware, and the documentation are both easily available and accessible.

Summary

With this, we are at the end of this chapter and the end of this book.

We hope you really enjoyed our time together and now have some solid confidence in your skills as an Alexa Skills Jedi.

Also, we hope that you have a good idea of what kinds of categories and skills are available in the Alexa Skills Store, why some of the skills do better than others, and which niche categories you can focus on when designing your next skill.

With all that information at hand, we cannot wait for you to publish your next skill. If you build something cool, drop us a line.

Other Books You May Enjoy

If you enjoyed this book, you may be interested in these other books by Packt:

Hands-On Chatbots and Conversational UI Development
Srini Janarthanam

ISBN: 978-1-78829-466-9

- Design the flow of conversation between the user and the chatbot
- Create Task model chatbots for implementing tasks such as ordering food
- Get new toolkits and services in the chatbot ecosystem
- Integrate third-party information APIs to build interesting chatbots
- Find out how to deploy chatbots on messaging platforms
- Build a chatbot using MS Bot Framework
- See how to tweet, listen to tweets, and respond using a chatbot on Twitter
- Publish chatbots on Google Assistant and Amazon Alexa

Building Bots with Microsoft Bot Framework
Kishore Gaddam

ISBN: 978-1-78646-310-4

- Set up a development environment and install all the required software to get started programming a bot
- Publish a bot to Slack, Skype, and the Facebook Messenger platform
- Develop a fully functional weather bot that communicates the current weather in a given city
- Help your bot identify the intent of a text with the help of LUIS in order to make decisions
- Integrate an API into your bot development
- Build an IVR solution
- Explore the concept of MicroServices and see how MicroServices can be used in bot development
- Develop an IoT project, deploy it, and connect it to a bot

Leave a review - let other readers know what you think

Please share your thoughts on this book with others by leaving a review on the site that you bought it from. If you purchased the book from Amazon, please leave us an honest review on this book's Amazon page. This is vital so that other potential readers can see and use your unbiased opinion to make purchasing decisions, we can understand what our customers think about our products, and our authors can see your feedback on the title that they have worked with Packt to create. It will only take a few minutes of your time, but is valuable to other potential customers, our authors, and Packt. Thank you!

Index

CPSIA information can be obtained
at www.ICGtesting.com
Printed in the USA
LVHW101629050119
602880LV00005B/16/P